Testimonies from the workshop and the book "Become a $uper Seller".

"This sales book has changed my life, this and the workshop have helped me to develop a better relationship with my family and with the people I have around me." Sergio Castilla, Colombia

"I am amazed by the knowledge I have received from the sales machine workshop that can be applied in my life. Above all, in the personal field I was able to discover many things about my abilities and fears and to be assertive in my interpersonal and professional relationships. "Juan David Zapata, México, DF

"Excellent Sales Machine training. Versatility will be my goal. ", Jacqueline Montoya, Publik Company, Colombia

"The best personal and business training along with the book of $uper Seller .... The opportunity to have a life change! "Adriana López, Chihuahua, Mary Kay

Here you can check the testimonials on Facebook:

Here you can check testimonials on YouTube of the sales machine workshop:

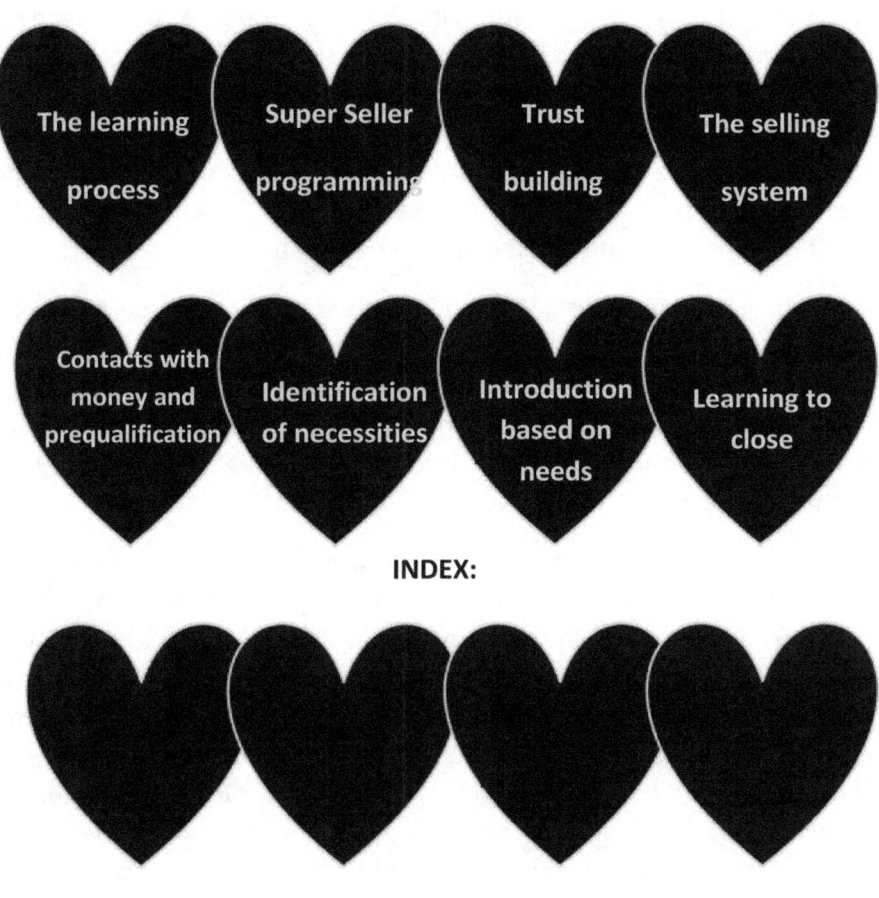

The learning process

Super Seller programming

Trust building

The selling system

Contacts with money and prequalification

Identification of necessities

Introduction based on needs

Learning to close

INDEX:

Why did I write the $uper Seller book?

Knowing how to sell is the most important skill that any person must have in order to be successful nowadays, talking about business, family, relationships with couples, children, parents, at school, at work and everywhere. Knowing how to sell is an art that is the oldest of all times and yet there is an aberration in this issue due to the negative programming in society. The detail is that this negative programming that sellers have haughty behaviors, little integrity, profiteering or whatever names we want to call has increasingly complicated the art of selling, but at the same time is still the best paid skill in the industry. Even more if you know how to use the sales tools in every part of your life, it becomes pleasant and much less complicated.

The important thing is to understand that we sell all the time, whether we like it or not is what we spend doing all the time, we sell to our partner that we love him or her, to our children to behave well, to our clients our products or services, to our parents that we are grownups, to our boss if you have a job that your job is well done, how we dress, the clothes we wear, how our body looks, the way we talk, etc.

So, it's better to learn to sell professionally and using proven tools that will make your life easier and above all you can have a better remuneration in whatever your profession, business, product or service you offer. Remember that we are selling all the time and nobody has taught us professionally to do it; not even in school still if you have done a master's degree, I am sure you did not learn the tools and if you learned them, you never used them properly, so this is your opportunity to take your performance to a next level because this book is practical, there is little theory and many tools that you should only use constantly, because as a salesperson we need to be constantly raising our capacity with proven tools.

So, I congratulate you on this important step and I am sure that like me, learning to sell will open the necessary doors to be able to have a spectacular life in every aspect.

David Gaona

You Tube video from the introduction of the CIPASA sales system:

Who do I have to thank for this book?

Thanks to all my University of the Street team and my family that is my inspiration, but especially I want to thank my beautiful mother who was the one who raised me in every way, she taught me to sell, to be disciplined with my physical activity, to be a warrior in life. That she, since I can recall, has been an example of struggle, devotion and especially a super seller who never gives up.

Why do I need to use selling tools?

The learning process

1

"If you want to change someone's life teach them to use a tool." Buck Misterfuller

1. Why should you be open?

2. Which are the three most dangerous words?

3. How to know if you really know?

4. Which is the passive way of learning?

5. Which is the active way of learning?

6. How to become an expert?

7.$uper Seller Powers

What is the learning process?

What you are going to learn in this book are tools, this book is 80% practical and 20% theoretical, we are going to assume that your task is to break a wall and I am going to teach you how to use a hammer, drill, hammer drill and even a demolishing machine to be able to break through that wall. It is similar as what you are going to learn, but with the sales and the need to become a $uper Seller, you will use a series of tools and techniques which will lead your level of income and your life in general to improve considerably, since remember that sales are used in all aspects of life.

POWER = Information + Action

$uper Seller Powers

In this book I'm going to teach you powers so you can become a $uper Seller, but I want you to understand, that powers are given with more information and action, in each chapter I'm going to put you to action, you'll have to work hard with the information you have and you will acquire supernatural powers that will differentiate you from any person, you will have a standard of living that very few people have, so please put yourself to work for your super powers with a lot of discipline.

First of all, what you have to do is unlearn many concepts and of course change some or many habits that haven't allowed you to advance enough and above all be open to understand that if you are not getting the results you expect or want, then you have to be open to learn how to use new tools and improve your habits to become a $uper Seller.

"The most important thing is to **unlearn** something that hasn't worked for you and **learn** what from now on **will change your life.**" David Gaona

Why should you be open to learn more?

The three most dangerous words in our language are "I know this", so if your brain at one point in this book begins telling you that you already know this, the first thing you are going to do is tell your brain to be quiet and to let you keep reading, then focus in doing the exercises to use the tools given in this book. Remember that when the "I know this" appears; it stops the learning process and blocks your brain creating a barrier and denying you the ability to obtain any valuable information.

Which are the three most dangerous words?

How to know if you really know?

The best way to know if someone really knows is with the results that they obtain. For example, someone who really knows about business is not precisely because they have studied a master's degree in business at a prestigious university or that they have worked as an employee in a company. The only way to evaluate their, ability in business is: How much money obtained by those businesses is in that person's banking account?

Last point, it is not the theory that person knows, nor the studies, not even the books, it is the results obtained from its business. So if you want to evaluate someone's business ability, tell them to show you their financial statements, if you really want to know if someone is an expert or really knows how to sell is the same process, you have to ask: How much do you sell daily or weekly? The same goes for the health and wellness topic, How do you know if the nutritionist or the weights instructor know what they are doing?, of course their fitness and the fiscal condition of their bodies and the amount of exercise they can resist.

It is as simple as this; the only way to know if you really know about any topic is if you are living according to the theory, you have to be a living example.

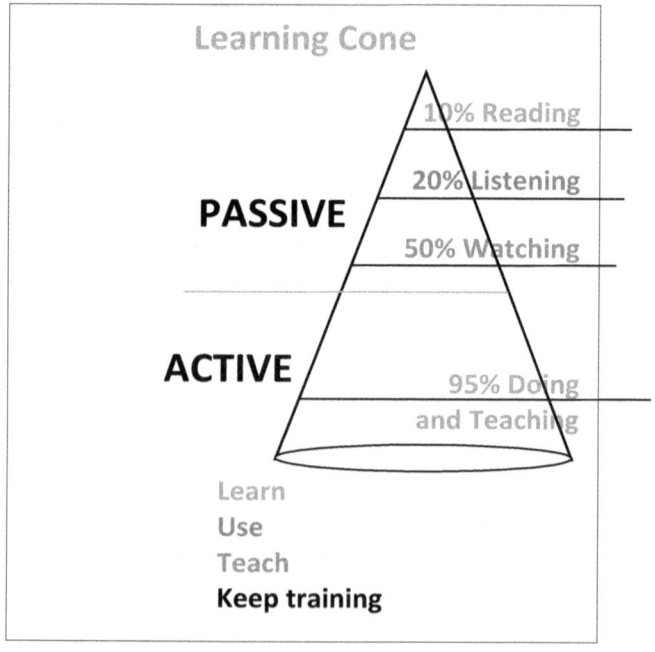

What is passive communication?

Expert

12

The Learning Cone explains pure statistics, the first part of the cone is what is known as passive learning or passive communication, it states that if you read any type of information such as a sales book you may only remember 10% of the information after 2 weeks, you might think that you learn more or less, but remember that what we are showing are averages only. If you differ, try to remember the last book you read and tell me what percentage of the information you are able to remember? It is most likely between 5 and 15%.

We learn 20% of what we hear, this means that after 2 weeks we only remember this little percentage, if you want to test this; Do you remember any conference or talk you have been in during the last year? The safest thing is that you say yes but you might only remember between 15 and 25% of the information you heard, or you can also do the test trying to remember the last classes of your master's, high school or university.

We learn 50% of what we see, this means that after 2 weeks on average we remember half of the information we observe, this is one of the most effective methods of passive communication, if you want to educate effectively either your children, employees or students the best way is by example, children, as well as adults learn more by example than with a conference or a book. Your children and employees are example of your actions, so this is one of the most effective ways to educate someone.

How to know if you are an expert?

As you have been able to realize either you have read, listened to lectures, attended courses or that you have seen your parents do something all your childhood does not mean that you know, you only have some information about it, but this does not determine if you really know or not, the results are what determine whether a person is an expert on the subject or not.

That is why it is so important that you understand that formal school is only a small step in professional training because in there, communication and education are passive. They never teach us to use information in real life and the cruelest thing is that doing well in traditional school is never going to assure you have success in real life. How many people you know who were excellent students and still earn $ 1,500 dollars per month? Or that they still remain unemployed.

However, knowing how to sell is a guarantee of success in your personal and work life as long as you maintain a good balance in your physical, spiritual and emotional state. As you were able to analyze the traditional school is focused on passive communication, so many who go to school (including me) do not gear with the system because we all learn differently, for example, I learn by doing and in school 90% of the information is reading, writing and listening so you must already imagine the heat shock that is for many of us going to school and why others were doing very well in there.

In the second part of the triangle there is active communication, and this is where you may become an expert. There are 4 simple steps, you have to learn the information or always have a summary in mind, you do not have to be a $uper genius to be able to know it by heart, there is mnemonics, which helps you learn with acrostics (it is a poetic or normal composition where the first, middle or final letters of each verse or sentence, read vertically, form a word or a phrase) and some other tools with which it is much simpler. The second step is that you have to use it, if you are paying attention I never say understand it, you just have to use it, what I'm going to give you in this book are tools is like a hammer to throw a wall, you just go and use it which avoids wanting to understand everything, the understanding comes after the practice. Once you start using it, which is where the traditional school falls short, your learning curve begins to accelerate. Even if there is something that you do not agree with or that you do not understand very well, the main task is to use it, until you understand it.

The third step is to teach it, but for this it is vital that you use it and that you really become a living example, because I know many people who are walking libraries, but they have never used the information and logically by not using it, but by trying to teach they are turning people to the same students, employees or children, like clones that never use what they know. Remember that people learn more what they see in you than what you can say or put them to read, remember that your children or employees are an exact copy of your habits. A $uper Seller is a leader in every way and we teach $uper powers all the time.

I'll give you an example, I have a productivity consulting company www.iexito.com, where we help entrepreneurs achieve their goals in record time, with world-class tools from the Rockefeller system, the first evaluation we do to the entrepreneur is to know what hurts the company the most and why? Because the company is a reflection of the owner's habits, that simple.

So teaching involves many things and you have to know how to use the tools and even further to be a living example in order to teach.

The fourth step to become an expert is to re train constantly, I remember perfectly the day I took my first training that I paid from my pocket it was financial intelligence in the US, and I remember that the instructor told us that we would remember this training for the rest of our lives and probably more when we were financially free. I remember that voice perfectly because for more than 10 years I have been financially free, and it was 15 years ago that I took that course. The most important thing that I want to tell you is that the courses and workshops you take are going to stay with you, they are an investment. I take 1 course and I teach 2 per month, I have my training plan and I have a trainer who has been with me for more than 12 years, you have to retrain, in what? In everything, I train in sales, finance, leadership, investment, marketing, every 3 years I repeat the same courses to be an expert in the use of tools. That is why we also have a company where we teach courses www.ucalle.com, Train yourself with us! Here you can find a course taught by experts who really do and reflects in their pocket; we have the "The sales machine" workshop which is the experiential workspace of this book. Where more than 100,000 people have taken our courses and have been able to live radical changes such as increasing sales by 300% in 5 months, or achieving their ideal weight, opening their own business successfully, among many other results. And if you think I'm selling you, you're right! But this could not be a sales book as I have to lead by example. Train yourself!

"It is not what you know what **matters**, it is what you do with what you know what is going to really give you **massive results**." David Gaona

Now that you know what are the steps to become an expert, I will explain the 4 stages we go through in order to become experts in the use of tools, the first is Unconscious Incompetence, this is what happens to people who do not know that It is happening to them or why it is happening to them. Better called victims, they believe that everything happens to them because they have bad luck or because they were born without the skills or in poverty.

They think that they are destined to never succeed in something. Speaking of sales are sellers who do not sell and think that they were not born for that and that they do things, but without any result.

The second is called conscious incompetence following the example of those of us who are salesmen you know that you are failing at some part of the sale, as in the case of closures; we are going to assume that you are doing everything right, you make the contact, the client has the need, you make the presentation and the person wants to, but you cannot sell them. Why? You do not know how to close. You are aware, but you still cannot move forward, and you feel frustrated, in other words, you know about your weakness, but you cannot do anything about it.

The third is conscious competence, this stage is very fun, but it is a stage we are going to say is mechanical, you know what the tools are, you use them in the right situation, sometimes at the right time and sometimes not. But it is when you realize about the sales that you know all the steps, you have the right tools for the right situations and you just have to work with the right moments. You know how to attract contacts that have money and need, you know how to identify the needs of the clients, you know how to make the presentations, you know the closing strategies and when to use them, you know how to request payment and follow up, you ask for testimonies and referrals, but it still does not come out naturally.

At last, the fourth one is unconscious competence, this means that you become a $uper seller, you have all the tools and you know the right moments to use them, but in a natural and innate way you have $uper Powers, this starts happening after you make about 100 presentations using the right tools. A different example is like when you learn to play a sport and you have been training with the basics for almost a full year and the time comes for the match or competition and your body naturally starts using the movements according to the play in an unconscious way Everything flows because you are prepared and you have been training, you know what to do at the right time and in the right situation, this is the culminating moment of learning, but the most important thing is that you can always continue learning and become better at what you do; In the sales profession above all.

I always say that being a $uper Seller is like being a high performance athlete; it takes a lot of training to be able to become one of the best. This is where your $uper powers begin to manifest; everyone tells you that you have natural talent and gifts. It really is true, you have $uper powers.

Learning Requires Energy

You need to understand that learning, as well as selling, requires a lot of energy, this is a concept that most amateur marketers do not understand. The profession of sales is the most exhausting profession there is, apart from requiring constant learning, I always compare it to a high-performance athlete and if you do not prepare as such I am sure you are not getting the results you should get. In fact, I recommend you even hire a coach; I have a financial coach since age 22. If you want more information about coaching for companies we have something that can help you at www.iexito.com , Train with us!

Coming back to the issue of selling and learning requires a lot of energy, I'll give you an example, one of my main businesses is transportation, I have that business since I was 17, I started it when I was in college and I worked on that every day during weekends, after a Saturday and Sunday of 10 services I ended up really exhausted, but when I finished working I still had the energy to run to the "Cerro de la Silla" or go to play basketball or go to the movies. But now, although I feel that I am in better physical condition at 36 years old than at 17 after finishing a day of 5 sales appointments, I end up more exhausted than when I was working at the moving company and I am finished by 7 pm, but it is because of the emotional and energy consuming that each sales appointment is.

"So you need to comprehend that **selling, learning,** and casually **earning money,** require **a lot of energy**." David Gaona

So, for you to really stay etched and be an expert you have to be studying all the time with audios and with books. Go to seminars and trainings, but train with the best. Never skimp on your training because this is going to stay with you all your life, it is really an investment. I take courses in sales, leadership, administration, etc. At least 10 or 12 per year, it is very important that, even if you are an expert, you keep training. Remember that you are like a high-performance athlete, the best in the world keep at the top training every day. As my sports coach says:

"The **games** and the **negotiations** are **won** with what you do in your **free time**." Nacho Moreno

What you are going to learn in this book is 80% tools and 20% theory, this is what really works in real life and I tell you with this example: I had done 100 thousand dollars in a single appointment by using what I'm going to show you in here. What you're going to learn here are proven tools that I keep using and improving all the time I learned them and I'm still learning from the best in the world. Also, I want you to understand that if you want to change a person's life what you have to do is give tools instead of a lecture or a scolding, instead give them something they can use to do better.

"If you want to change someone's life teach them to use a tool." Buck Misterfuller

In fact, I want to invite you to take a course we give at the Street University called "Trainers in accelerated learning" that will help you to potentiate your skills as a coach and salesman, in there we show you how to teach in a very efficient way, I promise you that it will change your life, imagine being able to sell to thousands of people at the same time as the great coaches do. Do you want to learn this? You may contact us at www.ucalle.com. Train with us!

$uper Seller Powers

1. Mnemonics: learn to memorize, there are several very good brands you may even buy software that can help you, so you don't even have to attend classes.
2. Quick reading: This tool along with the knowledge of memorizing are the two main skills that will change your life.
3. Calendar of courses: Make a list of all the courses you want to enroll and plan to attend throughout the year, list all the ones you need to be a $uper seller, about leadership, administration and investment, remember to include those from www.ucalle.com.
4. Book of learning: Every time you learn something or read a book, you have to make sure that you write it down in your notebook so that when you

want to remember that information, you just need to go to that notebook.

5. Mental maps: these will help you make your notes in a more orderly and structured manner. Once you learn to use them, I assure you that your learning process will increase in a large proportion.

6. Assign study schedules: Preferably early in the day either at 5 or 6 in the morning or 10 to 11 at night, remember that the first thing you put in your head is what you will have for the rest of the day.

7. Rolling university: Make any moment one of learning, put on your cell phone, tablet or computer all audio books as possible, so you can access them when you have time. For me it is automatic, I get to the car and it's time to listen audio books, we have 10 of them at www.ucalle.com. You may also listen to classical music such as Mozart, Paganini, Chopin, Beethoven, etc.

POWER = Information + Action

Are you a $uper Seller?

$uper Seller programming

2

"Sales are a **transfer of emotion** over your product, idea or service." David Gaona

1.What are sales?

2.What is a $uper Seller?

3. Which decrees does a $uper Seller use?

4. How to program yourself to become a $uper Seller?

5. Why should you ask for help from the creator?

6. What is discipline?

7. $uper Seller Powers

What are the sales?

Sales are the transfer of an emotion over a product, service or idea. The description is too simple, so in order to become a $uper Seller, the first thing you have to do is to be an excellent switcher or inducer of emotional states, the first person you have to learn to turn on and turn off the emotion button is to yourself and then make that emotion transfer to the client. You have to work in getting yourself convinced in what you are doing, you have to be proud of being a salesperson and of dedicating yourself to this wonderful profession. There are different tools to help you sell yourself, you have to program your subconscious so that when you arrive to the sale with the client you are completely prepared and convinced.

"Sales are a **transfer of emotion** over your product, idea or service." David Gaona

I'll give you a fundamental statistic that only $uper Sellers know, the closing of the sale is made in the first and in the last 3 minutes in which you meet the customer. So, you have to prepare yourself in order that when you arrive to make the sale you have already won it, your subconscious brain has to be so programmed that when the client sees you, knows that you will help, inspire confidence and great strength.

Another point is that you understand that sales are the most important part of the company, without sales there would be no business, so you are in the most strategic position and without you there would be no results and there would be no money to pay employees.

"The **closing of the sale** is made in the **first and in the last 3 minutes** in which you meet the customer." David Gaona

Remember that the sales are the most important part of a business, without them the business wouldn't be business.

What is the pain and the pleasure in sales?

The decision of whether to buy or not, like everything in this life, is a result of whether the person, the situation, the company or the product that is being presented to us gives us pain or pleasure. We have a part of the brain called the reptilian brain that has not evolved for millions of years, it is our caveman brain and is the one that performs the main function of the brain that is to move away from pain and closer to pleasure. Everything we do was first evaluated by our brain and if it gives us pleasure you do it and if it gives us pain you avoid it at all costs. For example, there are many people who cannot get up in the morning, the main reason is that the brain sends a signal that sleep produces more pleasure than waking up to exercise.

"**Sales** as everything that we do, is evaluated by our brain by if it provides pleasure or pain." David Gaona

The first part that you need to understand is that if it is a pleasure for you to make sales, and your client feels that it's a hobby for you and you enjoy doing what you do, the second part of the sale is to look for whatever gives pleasure to your client and find a way to satisfy their needs at the same time. Remember that our brain seeks to do everything possible to avoid pain and sales is a transfer of emotion. We have a workshop that will help you with this issue called "the workshop of the Warrior", in this workshop you learn how to make pain and fear your allies, remember that they are teachers too, Train with us!

The story of the neighborhood curtains salesman

For me it has been a very complicated process, because I come from a family where sellers have a reputation of people who do not study and it is a bad thing to be in this profession, in fact I remember perfectly the story that my father told us: "If you keep getting bad notes, you're going to dedicate to sell curtains like the gentleman in the corner." I remember that I used to cry because I did not want to dedicate myself to sales, for me it was like a humiliation and I started studying because I wanted to make my dad feel proud and study engineering like he and several uncles had done it. And he always used the classic tale that if we did not study we would dedicate ourselves to selling curtains and blankets as the man who lived around the corner.

Who makes more profit an engineer or a salesman?

My way of thinking changed radically when I started to have a coach, because the first skill that he made me work on was sales, for me it was a terrible thing because my father always told me that sales was the worst profession that existed and only people who had nothing else to do was dedicated to them, that's when everything changed because my coach asked me: Who earns more in the company where you work? To which I replied the seller Victor Perez, I remember perfectly the anger with which I said the name. But undoubtedly, he moved me, he told me that the seller is who always earns more in a company and is the one who brings the money to the company. The first skill you must learn to be an entrepreneur is getting to know how to sell, if you are not able to sell the business does not exist, the second skill you must develop as an entrepreneur is leadership, third administration and finally investment.

So, the answer is that a salesperson earns more than an engineer. Therefore, I got into a multi-level business to learn the magic of sales and become a $uper Seller. It was here where my life took a radical turn, in 6 months I was already earning double. Why? Because as a professional or employee you are always selling, even if you do not like it, so learning to sell for me has been something that has made my results multiply considerably.

What do you need to do to enjoy selling?

You have to work so that selling becomes your hobby; this is the key to obtain pleasure in selling. I'll give you an example, I have my companies and in my spare time I like to spend time with my family I like to sell cars, properties, meet new people and customers, go door to door selling with my daughters, sell books, etc.

Everything that regards selling for me is a hobby, if I have free time the first thing I say is what can I sell?, I know it sounds a bit strange but my head is already so prepared for it that I do it automatically is the unconscious competence that I mentioned to you earlier. That is why it is important that you sell all the time, all the time you should be looking for new clients, so you do it as a hobby and not out of necessity; that you do it because it is really in your heart to help and you enjoy doing it.

"The key so that sales become successful, is that you do them as a hobby and not out of necessity." David Gaona

Another tool is the constant training, I program my trainings month after month, at least I read a book per week and almost always I re-read them, also I listen to audios in my car all the time or when I exercise to be able to continue learning.

Remember that a high-performance athlete trains at least 6 hours a day, so a $uper Sales Person has to train at least 4 hours a day, make the time and schedule it. Now, if you really want to go to the next level then you have to hire a coach to help you reach levels you have never dreamed of, but make sure you train with the best or with someone who has already achieved what you want. Train with us!

"The myth that the **great seller** is born is wrong, a seller is made as **athletes**, you are born with certain **abilities**, but you develop the rest." David Gaona

Since you know that being a top seller is a matter of becoming an expert in the use of tools, it is important that you also have a clear goal. You must know how much you want to earn per year, per month, per week and per day. You have to be clear about your goals, not only in the field of money but also in all aspects of life, then one of the main tasks you will have is to make your goals. List 50 things you want to achieve in 5 years, write it in a notebook specially dedicated for your goals, it is important that you keep them close to you always, and also try to do them with the SMART + methodology. Your goals must be specific, measurable, achievable, results-oriented, time-bound and positive. The method of putting all your goals in writing is one of the most powerful that exist. Make your list and every day re write the most important, if you want more information on how to structure your goals you can go to www.ucalle.com and buy the audio book of "how to crystallize your dreams" so that you do it in a more structured way, Train with us!

Another tool is to work on your clothes and your physical condition. Why? It is very simple: So that you can program yourself positively. The colors and the clothing that you use is 70 to 80% of the sales because it is how you will feel, the colors are an activator of emotions, and there are 4 colors that the experts advise to provide a positive impact on sales. Black, blue, gray and white. All of them are colors that reflect seriousness and give a touch of knowing what you are talking about, remember that colors make your emotion change and also change the emotional state of the person to whom you are selling. It may sound a little hard to believe, but understand that the brain thinks of images and colors, let's make an example, close your eyes and think of an apple; surely you thought in red, green or yellow, what our brain does is to relate the colors with certain things that have happened to us in life, so if you want to make a good impression and avoid causing pain to your clients then make sure to use the adequate colors.

I have a client to whom the pink color causes a total aberration on him and that just seeing somebody in that color puts him in a bad temper, I remember that once we had got into confidence he told me: "It's great that you're not the typical salesman who uses bulging colors because I do not buy them anything. "

Now with this information you are wondering, do I have to stop using colors like red, pink, orange and yellow? The answer is yes, remember that each of those colors has something meaningful subconsciously to the other person, for example you wear red this is the color of passion and if you are a woman and you go with a man you are awakening passion subconsciously, it is the same with tight clothes or necklines regardless of gender, remember that our reptilian brain is the one that makes the decisions of our head and seeks to bring us closer to pleasure, so if you want your client to focus more on your product or service, you need to watch the clothes and the colors you wear. As well as odors that you dismiss, this is critical, remember that because of this you can win or lose a customer, always look for your smell to be barely perceptible and that is the least showy.

Your fitness is something that as a $uper seller you must constantly take care of, as I have told you throughout the book being in this beautiful profession is similar to being a high performance athlete, remember that having 5 sales appointments in one day is much more exhausting (not only I say it but several of the best coaches in sales in the world) that making 4 to 5 hours of hard exercise. So here the task is that you assign one or two hours every day to exercise so that you have the endorphins to be able to hook your client, and the energy to be able to transfer the emotion of your service, idea or product.

In order to make all these tools a conscious competence, the key is to use them every day for at least 3 months in a row. There is something that we use in University of the Street the company of education for entrepreneurs of which I am owner that is called the hour of POWER. It consists in every day before 6 in the morning you need to do the following:

Prepare yourself: Wake up and do 100 push-ups and 100 squats.

Orison: Pray and thank for everything that there is to come and for what you already have.

Weekly agenda: Define your daily agenda and make it a week in advance.

Elaborate a green juice of chard, cucumber, lemon and celery.

Re write your 5 main goals in a notebook every day.

"You have to become so **attractive** that **people seek out for you** instead of you looking out for clients." David Gaona

Our brain has about 70,000 thoughts per day, 99% percent dominated by our subconscious. How many thoughts do you really master during the day? There really are very few on average 5 or 6, with the use of tools and establishing habits you can master many more of these thoughts. The hour of power as every tool that comes in this book has as its main objective to help you meet your goals as quickly as possible.

Remember a $uper Seller is the one who knows how to dominate himself and can change or transfer the emotion of a product, idea or service. In this book we have seen several tools for you to master your emotional state, but here are 3 steps of mental warm-up that you should do before each sale:

1. Control your breathing, you can even do meditation (I recommend the Silva method), also use special inspirational music for sales, a song that as soon as you hear it, I reminds you of a very special moment, for example one of the songs that I use before a sale, a basketball game or some important negotiation is the song "Simply the best" by Tina Turner, because it reminds me when I played college basketball at the Tecnológico de Monterrey and it was the song they played during the presentation of the team at the beginning of the games. Those types of songs are what you should use.

2. Make an anchor-type movement that as soon as you do it makes you remember all the good things you've achieved, for example I like to touch my heart with my palm, every time I do that, I remember all the championships I've won, of the sales in which I earned large amounts of money, of the courses and the people I have helped, of my family, makes me vibrate when I tap my chest, you can use this movement or take a leap or something that will help you raise your energy and enter into a winning state.

3. What you eat is essential, I have the routine in my hour of power of being able to take a green juice every day, I even take it at night because it makes me feel very good, remember that to be a super seller your energy must be very high and remember that sales is a transfer of

emotion or energy. The green juice will help you stay active, it will help you to concentrate the energy in the client, listen to it and in the presentation instead of the digestion, 80% of the energy of the human body is used in the digestion.

Remember that your $uper powers are going to activate as you take care of your body and improve your habits. There comes a time that when you improve the number of blessings they start to flow like a river and that is when you become a $uper Seller.

"The **difference** between a $uper Seller and a seller from the bunch, is the correct use of the basic selling **tools**."
David Gaona

How to turn from a cave man into a $uper Seller?

Sales are made by a transfer of emotions, so the control of these will determine the probability of success. The brain is divided into two, subconscious and conscious, and 98% of decisions are made by the subconscious. So, for the most part, the programming that has been introduced to us from 0 to 10 years old is the one that makes the decisions for us. So, we're going to have to work on reprogramming that negative programming to exchange it for the programming of a $uper Seller.

The main function of the brain is carried by our reptilian brain or better called the hypothalamus. This main function is to **get away from the pain** and get closer to the pleasure, imagine that you are a caveman from the prehistoric era, the only thing that our brain could do at that time (it always does) was to run to preserve our existence. The hypothalamus does not think it only carries out its main function.

So, the first thing we are going to work on is that your subconscious brain starts to like sales, that you feel the need to sell, since most of us as children we have been programmed in a negative way about sales.

What do you recall people telling you about salespeople or sales when you were a child? Even today there is an aberration for those of us who dedicate ourselves to this exciting and persistent profession. These were some of the phrases that are said about salespeople:

1. You dedicate yourself to sales because you did not study.

2. You had bad grades and that's why you dedicated yourself to sales.

3. There is no work for you, so you have to sell.

4. Sales are poorly paid.

5. Sellers are thieves.

6. Sellers cheat.

7. The sellers are carefree.

So logically what your brain does is that when the moment of the sale arrives, you feel pain, then you restrain yourself from making the call, the schedule, getting up early, dress well, exercising, etc....

To express it better: I call it the caveman that all of us have inside, that negative programming that we have since children and that doesn't let us go on, that restrain us and prevents us from pain that someone says something because we dedicate ourselves to sales, or the fear of being rejected and receive the terrible NO that is so fearful in sales.

Once you find that sales are scary and painful then you have to start doing things and, above all, change your thoughts to become a $uper Seller and program your hypothalamus so that from now on sales bring you pleasure. I will give you a set of decrees that you must start using every day to program your subconscious as a $uper Seller:

The decrees of a $uper Seller

I AM a $uper Seller.

I always help my clients and they always recommend me because of my excellent service.

I AM an excellent problem solver.

I always enjoy selling.

I AM a money magnet.

I always attract clients and people that want to do business with me.

I think that everybody has to win.

There are 7 steps that you have to take to program yourself as a $uper Seller. You have to understand that first you have to become and then you will have the results. First you act as if you were a $uper Seller and then your brain is going to start converting your caveman into a $uper hero. But first you have to change the way you speak, here I am providing you with some decrees so that you start repeating them every time you wake up and during your whole day. Repeat them constantly and make them part of your daily environment.

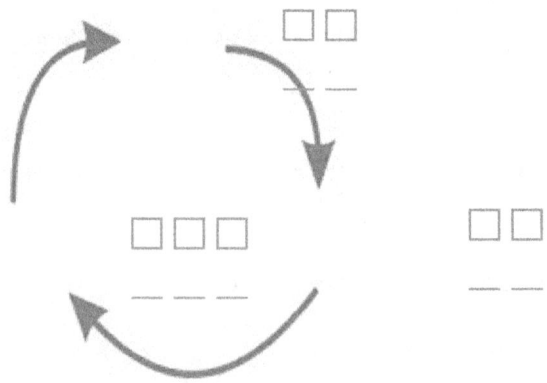

What do you need to do to program yourself as a $uper Seller?

1. Dress as a $uper Seller and use decrees all the time. Feeling that you are a successful person is in great part determined by the way you dress and the way you talk, as my coach says: "If you listen to a person talk for 5 minutes you may realize how the results of that person are going to be for the rest of their life."

2. Go to a sales or personal growth training seminar at least once every two months. Most of the salespeople omit this step or give it little importance, but the training for me is the difference between earning one thousand dollars or a hundred thousand dollars. Train yourself, and never spare, I take the same seminars every 2-years, so I can keep growing as a person. Train with us!

3. Use $uper Seller vocabulary, words program you for success or failure, you have to be very careful in every word that comes out of your mouth because your results are going to depend on that, use a sophisticated use of words, but adaptable at the same time, in order to do that you have to learn words that may be used according to each situation. Have a list of words for a $uper Seller.

grateful

please

thank you

health tha   I owe to you   thanks

tha   money

           I can do it

nks

nk   I love you blessings

     a

you   glad

    lot

                love

4. Read about sales at least one hour daily and listen to audio books for 1 hour also. You have to turn yourself in a rolling university, buy as much sales and personal growth audiobooks and books as you can, learn a new language while you are in your care, make sure that every time you get into your car you have something to learn, that is how I have learned to speak four languages, in my car and my traveling. It is also important that you have a library at home, design a special place for your learning.

5. Surround yourself only with friends and people that make you a better person. You are the average of the five people closer to you and there has to be in the top of your mind, as the old saying tells: "The one that walks with wolves to howl is taught." Be careful to whom you spend your time with, carefully pick your friends, your partner, your trainer. Make a list of people who are going to make you do better. Change your environment, rearrange your room as the one a $uper Seller should have. You have to make the environment inspire you to change, so that you can have the results the environment as well as the people that surround you have everything to do. Hang pictures that

inspire you, have a clean room, have quotes or decrees all around your room.

6. Hire a trainer specialized in sales. The only ones that have trainers are entrepreneurs and the world class athletes, if you wish to evaluate your level of income and of throughput then you have to hire someone that helps you to win what you have never been able to, in the same case if you are an athlete or as a sales person that is mostly the same. Make sure you train with the best. Train with us!

7. You have to celebrate every win you get, it doesn't matter if it is big or little you have to jump out of joy every time you move forward, this is going to make your brain to subconsciously begins giving pleasure to every step forward, celebrate every detail as never, this is something that only the high performance athletes and salespeople   and celebrate other peoples al:

Why should we have an accomplishments list?

What you are going to do now is a list of achievements with the 5 most important things you have done in your life. They are things that in your heart you know that they had cost you work but they make your heart vibrate, an example might be that you finished high school, having worked in such company, start your own business, have done a masters, a trip that you have done, to have bought a house, 5 things that you have celebrated at that moment with a lot of pride.

One of the keys to becoming a $uper Seller is that when you are very low in energy or you have some defeat you must ask yourself 4 questions that we will see more in detail further in another chapter, but the first one is: What happened? I recognize that I feel sad because I did not sell to this person, or I feel disappointed, I feel frustrated, you have to find the feeling that troubles you at that moment, the second is: What does work? You always must see what are the good things that you have in life, in a defeat you always do good things and a part of that you have to remember the good things you have done in general. This is where you need to remember the 5 achievements you have had, these will make you feel better just by remembering them. This question will make the defeat not hurt so much and remind you that you can do things better. Then you ask yourself, what did not work? This is where you must make a work plan. At last you need to ask yourself: What did I learn and what am I going to do differently? With this last question is when your head should start to revolutionize and start thinking about what is going to happen the next time.

Why should you have a special area for trophies?

Being a $uper Seller is very similar to being a high-performance athlete, as an athlete you have competitions, you have trainings, every day you have games and there are constant recognitions, like $uper Seller, you have presentations, you have expos, you have trainings and every day there are tests and recognitions. In fact, I can tell you that I get tired more by having a full day of sales than by exercising all day. Why? For all the emotions that are handled in sales, in fact, it is said to be 5 times more exhausting.

Then as a $uper Seller you have to own your trophies and recognitions area, this place must mean something to you, it must be that special place that when you just observe it you begin to feel very powerful. It must also be within reach of other people so that they know what you have achieved, not with the desire of presumption if not with the objective that when you feel low of energy or you are going through a defeat (as $uper Seller you will go through many), it will take you less time to recover your energy, also other people may also help you get out of that hole.

It is important that you understand that as a $uper Seller you need to stay with the highest energy always to be able to transfer your excitement about your product or service to thousands of people, so make sure you always give yourself luxuries or prizes. You must learn to treat yourself well, because in the sale you are the most important person.

Who is the most important person?

You are the most important person and you need to understand that, in order to become a $uper Seller you have to treat yourself well, you have to become so later you can have, remember that sales are a transfer of emotions and energy. So how is it possible not to take care of yourself and be able to close a sale? Well it has a very little probability, you have to treat you well and take care of yourself. You must exercise, eat a lot of fruits and vegetables (I recommend the tropology for a $uper Seller nutrition plan), drink 2 liters of water at least, you need to make your body and your character gain a lot of energy so you can transfer it to thousands of people, this is why its fundamental for you to take care of your body, mind and spirit. Sleep for 6 hours at least, meditate, remember that as salespeople we are exposed to a lot of parties and temptations like alcohol and other bad habits, but you are a $uper Seller and you are different, if you are going to attend a party take care of yourself and don't drink or drink the least possible, take care, take care of your body, your mind and your spirit and your reputation will take care of itself.

"**You** are the most **important person** and you need to get it, to become a **$uper Seller** you have to **treat yourself well**, you have to become in order to get, remember that sales are a **transfer of emotion and energy**" David Gaona

Why should you ask for the creator's help?

The truth is that we have to understand that we will always need divine help above all because we, as sellers, are soldiers of God, our goal is to serve and help our fellow human beings, so it is not superfluous to ask for help from the creator so that everything goes well. So I will share a prayer that I use every day to connect with my creator, read it before falling asleep and after waking up.

$uper Seller Prayer

My Lord, Creator of all things, thanks for always helping me keep my goals in mind.

Thank you for the ability to take advantage of my opportunities and teach me how to conquer with words and to thrive with love.

Thank you for helping me to live today as if it were the last and to guide my words so that they are fruitful and to help me discipline in order to never give up.

Thank you for opening my eyes to see every opportunity and for enriching me with good habits and for giving me patience and persistence to achieve each goal that I set for myself.

Thank you for helping me to sell more of my products and services, either by phone, online or in person and to do it in a simple and fluid way because my clients and prospects answer me easily and constantly look for me to obtain more of my products.

Thank you for helping us to sell more and more of our products and with them to help more and more people and to open more and more doors and provide us with more markets around the world.

Thank you for helping us to increase sales with our current customers and to increase our customer base in a smooth, easy manner and by recommendation.

Thank you for helping us meet and exceed the needs of our customers and that they become our best sellers due to our excellent service.

I thank you for everything you give me and what is yet to come because I know that I owe to you all the success and that's why I thank you and execute every action knowing that you guide me in every step.

To me this world is designed very fairly, everything behaves similar to nature, what do I mean by this? If you are planting lemon seeds, what is going to happen is that after a period of time you will start to see that a lemon tree will grow and if you keep taking care of the tree, providing sunlight, water, talking beautifully (Yes, you have to talk nice!), you take care that weeds do not grow, you put fertilizer, you give it water again, it is still sunny, you keep talking nice (if you notice, I keep emphasizing that you talk beautifully to it), then after about 3 years you start to see that it gives you one or two lemons, I'm talking to you from experience, (I just planted a tree in my backyard). So after a period of time that you plant in the business and sales scenario you will see results, but only after doing things every day, making calls, reading, studying, exercising, making new contacts, to have made many presentations.

It is going to get to a point that it starts flourishing. But if in this moment you are earning a thousand dollars per month instead of a thousand dollars per hour, I'm coming really harsh but you deserve it!

If they are paying you a thousand dollars is because you are able to solve type 1 problems, then life is really fair, you plant you harvest, then if you want your income to grow you have to start solving type 2 problems so that they pay you two thousand dollars, but you need to understand that in order to turn from a type 1 person to a type 2 there is going to be a lot of pain and growth because you need to solve bigger problems, it is not the same to solve the problem of one person than from two people and this is exactly what happens if you want to obtain more income or to sell more, because the problems that you are going to solve are going to increase. So prepare yourself to grow.

"Remember that if you want to **earn more** you have to **solve other people's problems** in a more efficient way." David Gaona

Now once you are able to solve type 2 problems, type 1 problems become opportunities, but only after you have overcome the pain and pressure, once you are able to solve type 2 problems everything changes. But there are always type 3 problems and you were not used to them. Those problems if you are type 2 and for which they pay you two thousand, you see them as huge and impossible to solve, those type 3 problems are always an opportunity to grow but always through growth and pressure, so you need to know that if you want to grow up and earn more you have to solve bigger problems and by then by natural law (you plan a lemon seed then you harvest a lemon) you are going to obtain better income for your services.

Let me propose an example I charge 3 thousand dollars per hour of advisory, Why?, because the company that hires our services knows that it is going to obtain more than 3 thousand dollars if it hires us then the client is willing to pay because they know that we are going to spare them a lot more than what they are investing. We solve the problems of tens of millions of dollars and that's why we charge what we charge.

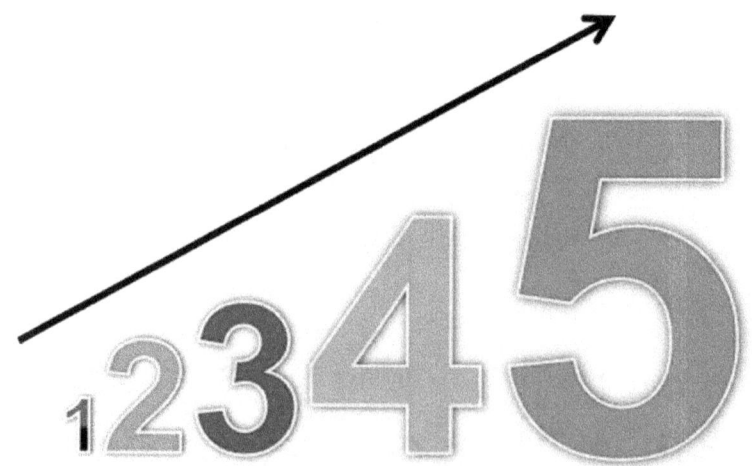

"It comes a time that **with training** the problems stop being **problems** and become **opportunities**." David Gaona

The more problems you solve, the more earning you are going to obtain, then you must become an expert problem solver and as the graphic below shows, if you solve other people's problems in an efficient way then you have the possibility to become really rich as Emmerson says:

"You are directly **compensated** by the **value** that you grant to the **market**." Emmerson

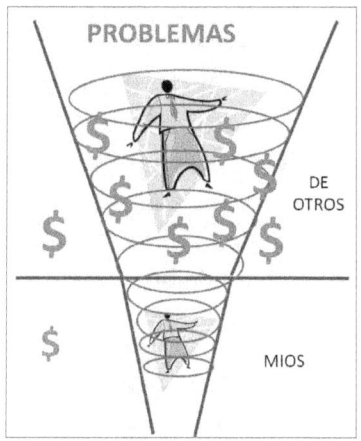

As long as problems exist remember that you are alive, thank your creator for the opportunity and ask him to turn you into a better person so you can solve more and bigger problems; never ask him to solve the problems for you, ask him to grant your health and strength to solve even bigger problems each time.

It is about grabbing and solving the problem every time you have one in front of you, focus in becoming better and you are going to notice how the universe is going to provide you with the tools to solve this problem and even bigger ones.

"Never ask your **creator** to solve the **problems** for you, ask him to grant your **health and strength** to solve even **bigger** problems each time." David Gaona

What is the importance of discipline?

To become a $uper Seller and solve a lot of problems you need to have discipline, it is doing what you need to do without minding if you want to do it or not, not even how the weather is in order to accomplish your goals with integrity, this is what makes the difference between an average salesperson and us, we make thing happen, we seek all of our goals and never stop, we are different, we arrive first to our appointments, we are training constantly, we are the ones who are always pushing for what we want and do whatever we need to do to accomplish it. We never give up, it might happen that we do not win all of our battles or always close a sale but we always give our best and are $uper disciplined.

"Discipline is doing what you need to do without minding if you want to do it or not, not even how the weather is in order to accomplish your goals with integrity. " David Gaona

Which is the first sell you need to make?

At sales there are always two types, the first one is to ourselves and the second one is with the client, the first sale is the most important one, to the extent that you sell to your own person the idea that you like your product, your service, you like yourself it is how your self-image or self-concept grows.

This self-image is as if you were outside your body and you are looking yourself from the outside, what would you say about yourself? would you like yourself?, would you buy from you? do you like your product? do you like your service? are you destined for success? If you answered no to one of those questions then you first need to work a lot in your self-concept you need to work in your self-confidence because the client observes, smells and feels this things.

Self-concept improves in order as our habits improve, exercising, reading, eating healthy, dressing well, everything that we have seen on this book, speaking about sales you first need to work into improving as a person and your self-concept and your sales are going to grow to the extent of how you do it.

In fact, if you want to take your self-concept to another level I want to invite you to our workshop "Think as a Champion" where they tech you to structure your goals and objectives as the big businessmen do it. Also, in this workshop we help you confront your fears in a very powerful manner we even walk though glass and fire. Here you can watch more about the workshop and request information. www.ucalle.com. Train with us!

Watch the testimonies from the workshop "Think like a Champion" in YouTube

The $uper Seller Powers

1. Make sales a hobby for you.
2. Read self-help books and use this book as the sales bible. Go to workshops, you may go to our workshops at www.ucalle.com and keep training, listen to audios while you ride in your car.
3. Clothing and fitness: The use of proper clothes in the right times is fundamental, you need to learn that you need to mimic your client, learn to wear the clothing they use or expect you to be using.

Exercise daily for at least 45 minutes, I request you complete at least 100 pushups and 100 squats daily, remember that you have the same or more wear that a high performance athlete and you require a lot of energy to win what you have dreamed.

4. Assing a special place in your room or the living room, use one wall to hang all the acknowledgements and diplomas that you have obtained, this is $uper important so when things are not going well you remind yourself that you are a champion, use decrees like "I am a $uper Seller" if you wish you may find more at the end of this book.

5. Prayer: Pray and talk to the infinite intelligence every day and make the creator become your partner, ask him to help you sell more and thank him for everything he gives you and what is already on the way.

6. Movies and Music: Have a list of positive songs that motivate you and make you feel good, also movies that make you change your state of mind once you watch them.

7. Written goals: have 50 things that you want to achieve, written in a special notebook, use the SMART+ methodology and have that notebook with you all the time. Re write your goals every day and this will help you keep them in mind all the time.

Why should you gain trust before selling?

Trust building

3

"Let's say that you have to become **your client's best friend.**" David Gaona

1.Which are your client's fears?

2.How do you turn someone unknown to someone you know?

3.How to turn someone you know into a friend?

4.How to turn a friend into a client?

5.How to turn a client into a seller client?

6.What is the compensation law?

7.$uper Seller Powers

How do you turn someone unknown to someone you know?

The first step is from unknown to known. Nowadays as Mr. Seth Godin along with other marketing and sales international experts say, it is becoming more different and interesting the art of influencing and helping people. Every year you have to innovate according to what the client is looking for, this is why you have to know that the trust building is not like few years ago, now with the use of technologies and all the information in the internet, the competition has become huge because now you can buy with just a click and the product is sent from China or the United States and it arrives in a matter of days, and there's also thousands of people offering the same product or service. This is why the first task in the 4 steps of building trust is to convert someone unknown into someone you know. This first instance is the most important of all; most of the time the salespeople take this step for granted even though is the most important of the four of them. You need to understand that only in a few times you are going to sell to someone unknown I think about 20% to 30%, for the rest you have to begin building a friendship relationship with your clients.

Is like when you begin a relationship with a couple, if you like the person you are going to go through a series of dates while you meet each other, then if both of you agree and after 5 or 6 times going out, it is probable that you begin a couple's relationship. Understand that after 5 dates at least!

What difference does it have with the relationship with a client? None, it is exactly the same you before making a sale you have to go through at least 20 or 30 dates on average so you can gain enough trust from your client. Not before, you have to keep that number in your mind and not look to sell, instead build trust to establish a long-term relationship.

"Let's say that you have to become **your client's best friend**." David Gaona

Which are the client's fears?

Remember that the clients have fears and you need to help them gain trust and in that way dissolve the fears that prevent them from buying from you. The fears are the following:

When a client asses a sales offer, a series of fears that condition it's decision begin to appear. Try to know them in advance and provide an adequate answer to increment the possibilities of closing the sale. We summarize them in here.

1. Fear of making a mistake. The principal fear of a client by the time of obtaining a product or service is not choosing correctly. To avoid it, analyze properly their needs and offer a right solution.

2. Fear of change. When the sale implies to change supplier or way of working, a resistance to change and nostalgia for the previous solution appears. Highlight the advantages that the new system brings.

3. Fear of having to work more. Very attached to the fear of change, is the fear that the purchase decision will complicate their life. Reduce it by making the transition as easy as possible and by providing good post-sales support.

4. Fear of paying more. Especially the inexperienced buyers may have the feeling that their ignorance supposes an extra cost. Provide ease by comparing your prices with other solutions.

5. Fear of commitment. Fears of change, cost overruns, etc. become worse when the purchase supposes commitments in the long term. A return or cancellation policy for dissatisfaction will dispel this fear.

6. Fear not to size well. It is also common to fear choosing a solution too big or too small for your needs, which you can combat by offering the possibility of changing it in the future.

7. Fear of being criticized. The buyer may also fear that their managers, partners, customers, etc. will question their choice. So give them arguments to defend their decision.

8. Fear of conflict. Finally, the customer can show resistance if the purchase supposes facing their old supplier. Discourage this idea by advising them to cancel his previous contract in a friendly way.

Why does a client stop buying?

The graphic above shows which is the first cause why a client stops buying, it is mostly because we provide a poor service because a lack of communication. This is the main cause, remember that the client has fears like any other person and on the extent in which you help their head overcome their fears this is when they are going to buy. They have to trust that they are going to obtain from you what they are expecting and that you are going to fulfill their needs regardless of what your product or service is.

How to turn someone you know into a friend and from a friend into a client?

The second step into trust building is to turn them into a fiend, after a series of 10 to 15 meetings a person or client is going to feel identified with you, remember that a person really feels interest that you are going to help them so make sure is as genuine as possible, think of when you have made a friend. How did you do it? Was it because you had common habits, hobbies interests, so work to make the other person feel comfortable with you, selflessly think of how to help them and make "click" with the other person.

The third step is to turn them from a friend to a client, after a number of meetings, calls, conversations, then begin the sale of your product or service, the first part and the first meeting were for you to gain the client's trust and for them to understand the value of what you are doing and that you want to stablish a long term relationship, here it is when you begin capitalizing that friendship with your products or services.

At this point you begin your presentations, you know where your is product or service going to help your friend, it might be in their personal life, business or where you see the opportunity to serve, so it's your obligation to satisfy those needs.

How to turn a client into a seller client?

The fourth step is to turn them into seller clients, once your friend becomes your client and you provide the service you would give to your best friend, then is when you can ask them to help you selling with other of their friends. You are going to notice that this same client is going to recommend you without you even asking, but it is important to highlight that you need to keep this friendship. The clients and fiends are lost because of lack of communication, so stablish a constant channel, I can't say daily, but at least something informal on a weekly basis, like a phone call, an email, and monthly a dinner or a visit to their office, maintain your clients the same way you maintain a friendship.

"**Clients** as same as **friends** are lost mainly because a **lack of communication**." David Gaona

As a $uper Seller this is the main tool, that you treat your clients as your best friends. If you are thinking that you don't have them, now is the time, you need to work in the relationship with the people around you, so your sales income increases. So you must understand that by law you are going to get a reward for the treatment you are giving to your clients.

What is the compensation law?

Did you know that there is an eternal law of compensation? In his essay about compensation the philosopher Ralph Waldo says: Every action has its reward, in other words, action and reward are combined in a dual manner. The compensation law may work to our benefit or in our damage according to our actions. Sooner or later the compensation arrives, maybe after several years, but the time of punishment or reward arrives. The punishment or the reward might arrive a lot of time after the felony or the good deed is done, but it will always come, because it accompanies it. Cause and effect, means and ends, seed and fruit, they cannot be separated, because the effect always blooms from the cause. There is always a third part in all of our deals. The nature and the soul of things take charge of the warranty of compliance of every contract, in which honesty can't lose. Each stroke must be paid. And the longer the payment is delayed; the better for those who expect it, since a compounded interest multiplied by itself is the proportion it uses to pay for that divine tribunal. The third and silent part is the invisible force that in its eternal action ensures that every contract celebrated with the world is fulfilled.

That is why the compensations of adversity appear clear to the understanding, after long intervals of time. As Emerson says,

"Every excess causes a defect, every defect causes an excess, there is no sweet that does not have some acidity, and no evil that does not contain something good. For everything that one has been deprived, another will have been won and for something that is won a similar loss occurs. If the assets of the fortune increase, at the same time the demands increase. There will always be some leveling circumstance that places the strong, the rich, the fortunate, essentially on the same plane as other men." Every thought that our mind emits, whether good or bad, will return to its time, greatly multiplied, to curse it or bless it according to its original nature.

"Every **excess causes a defect**, every defect causes an excess, there is no **sweet** that does not have some **acidity**, and no **evil** that does not contain **something good**." Emerson

It is a law of nature to grow says Emerson. In this regard he comments that such growth often encompasses adversities of many types, but these setbacks often serve to end some period of life that needed to be closed. Likewise, adversity interrupts certain ways of life and helps us develop new ones that may be necessary for our progress. The person who has been tempered in misfortune becomes a stronger being who can do more for himself and for others. That is why Napoleon Hill appropriately says "To every adversity corresponds an equivalent or greater benefit". And Víctor Hugo says: "Give the world the best you have and the best will return to you, because life is like a mirror, it only reflects what we give". John Wesley says: "Do all the good you can, in all the ways you can, in all the places you can, on every occasion that you can, to all the people that you can, and during all the time you can." They say that the Rotary's Motto is the following: "Give of yourself, rather than think of yourself".

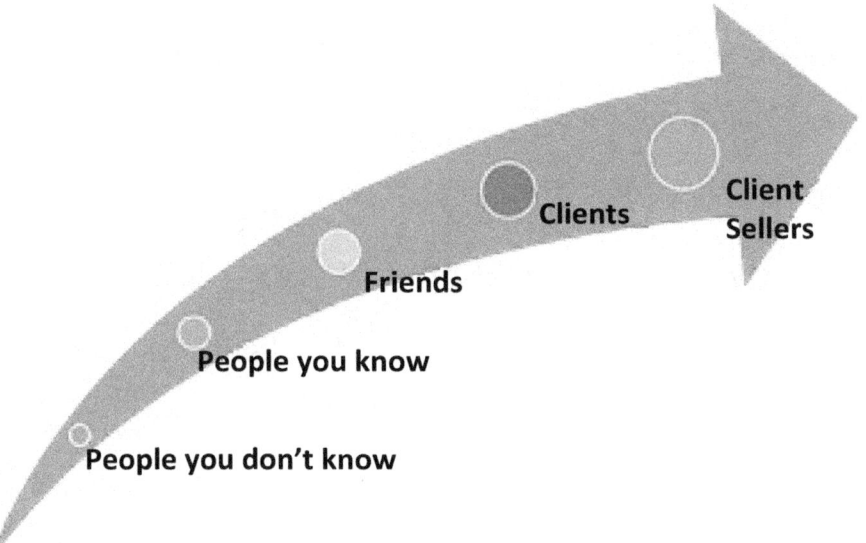

"Think that you are like an **additional resource** for your clients: a consultant, a counselor, a mentor, **a friend** and not **just a simple salesperson**."
Brian Tracy

Why are you an advisor?

Once the client knows that your objective is to help them they are going to look at you as their advisor, you are a support to them, a person they know they can trust not only are you going to sell this is going to turn you into their personal advisor, in their friend.

An advisor doesn't sell, its actions sell by itself; because is a person who cares for its client or for the person he or she advices, make sure your clients see you as an advisor.

"An advisor **doesn't sell, its actions sell** by itself." David Gaona

An advisor is a sales professional who:

1. Sees the clients as long-term customers.

2. Advises on the best solution for the client including sometimes over our products or services.

3. Is interested in customers and their companies.

Why do you have to become a product of your product?

One of the fastest ways to also generate confidence is that you are a fervent admirer of your product, there are many sellers who want to sell their product without even consuming or using it. This is something very incoherent and dangerous because people are very smart and your customers are even more, so how do you want to sell someone if you do not even believe in what you sell?

For example, if you sell Honda-branded cars and you use a Chevrolet, doesn't matter the reason that you are going to tell me this means that you do not really want your product, even more so your customer smells it, he knows that you do not believe in Honda cars, and you believe in Chevrolet cars, your probability of selling with this type of actions decreases.

You need to become a product of your product, you need to love what you sell, if they are lotions use them, if they are cars get your own car, if you provide a service you have to become an admirer of your product and become your own fan.

To the extent that you become a product of your product you are going to gain confidence and this is going to make you sell automatically.

I remember one time I was in a multilevel company, I had one person in my net who had 2 years working really hard, making daily presentations and couldn't make his business grow, he had never won more than 2 thousand dollars in his business, when I got to work with him I began questioning a lot of stuff, one of the main reasons he was not doing better is that he didn't use the product we promoted, I remember he got mad at me and told me he didn't have enough money, that the product was very expensive, he gave me all the objections his clients gave to him, until I could sell to him; I asked him to immediately buy the product, to which he denied, I told him either you do it or you do it, you need to understand that you haven't sold because you don't believe in the product.

He just told me, once I sold him, the product arrived within a week, he began consuming and by the next month he was earning almost 4 thousand dollars, the problem wasn't the lack of hard work it was that the seller didn't believe in his own product.

"In the extent to which you become the product of your own product you are going to gain confidence and this is going to automatically make you sell more." David Gaona

$uper Seller Powers

1. The sweetest word a person is going to listen to is their name, to gain trust or empathy with a person you are going to try to talk to them by their name, you have to say their name for at least in a minute, this is going to familiarize the person with you.
2. Shut up, that's right, you need to understand that the least you need to do to impress someone is to talk, instead you need to listen to what the other person wants to say, one of the main needs humans have is to be valued and listened to.
3. Make questions in order to begin the conversation, make sure you make them about what they are telling you, if they talk about soccer, talk to them about soccer, if they talk you about business then talk about business, it is important that he notices that you know about the topic.
4. Pay attention, zero distractions while talking to the person, avoid using cell phone or be messaging preferably turn it off while you talk, remember that nowadays we are very few people who really put 100% attention when engaging in a conversation so be a $uper Seller and make them feel that the conversation is the most important thing for you at that moment.
5. Do not seek to sell on the first meeting unless they ask, the sale is an art and you have to give yourself to wish, remember that a number of appointments must pass until you can sell to a stranger unless they ask, a $uper seller has patience.

6. Talk about what interests them, if you can investigate beforehand what are that person's interests, learn from their business, take a look around the office or your environment and talk about what you see around and ask questions.
7. Selflessly seek to help them, even with something simple but be honest, if you see that they have a very clean office, tell them, if you see that they like to dress well, it is important that you work on yourself so that when you say something good to someone it is said with a heart and with the intention of recognizing them. Do simple things, remember that God is in the details.

POWER =

Information +

Action

Why should you use a system to sell?

The selling system

4

"**The difference** between a **$uper Seller** and a **salesperson from the bunch** is the proper use of the basic **tools** in a sale." David Gaona

1. Which is the worst mistake in sales?

2. Which are the keys to attract a champion team?

3. How much does it cost to buy a client?

4. Which is the language of a $uper Seller?

5. What is the CIPASA system?

6. How did you do in the evaluation system?

7. $uper Seller Powers

Why use the CIPASA system?

The system that we are going to show you in here is a system that has many years working and is called **CIPASA**, it only has a few variations and adapting, it is improved according to my experience and thousands of presentations that I have done to my clients and of course after millions of dollars in profit. I need you to understand that $uper Sellers do this in a masterly way. First you need to understand that before getting to the selling system that never fails. First you must have a written sales plan; you must manage an annual budget. How much is your goal to sell by month from here to the end of the year? By product, by seller, by area, etc. That's where your goal as a salesperson begins.

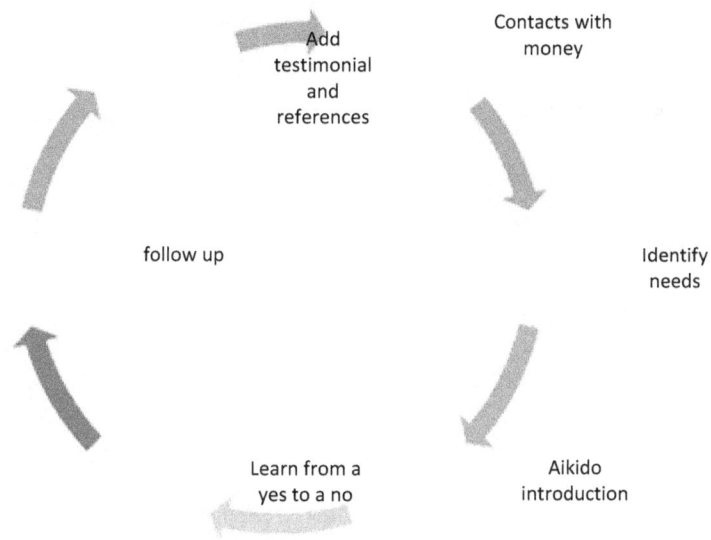

Which is the worst mistake at sales?

Most companies and amateur salespeople fail from the beginning because they do not have a written sales plan, this step is the fundamental one, this is where all the action plans, marketing, production, training, alliances, strategic planning are derived. This is the head of the company and what gives direction to most departments and in case you do not have a company is where you give yourself direction to where you want to go and where you see yourself a year from now .

Now if you really want to start like a professional then do a strategic plan of 5 years, answer the following questions:

How do I see myself as a seller in 5 years?

How much would I like to win?

What products would I like to sell?

As a company:

How much would I like to sell?

With what products?

In what markets?

How many employees?

Make a complete plan and the corresponding strategy, as if you had a magic wand, now if you have doubts about how to make a strategic plan, then I recommend that you hire someone who can help you. In www.iexito.com we can help you to give shape to this plan, we have coaching for entrepreneurs, or you can go to a workshop with us where we can guide you. Train with us!

Now that you have your plan of how much you are going to sell in 1, 5 and 10 years then you have to work on systematizing the sales process, find out what are the key procedures within the company or your process if you are an independent salesperson. There are usually 7 processes:

1. Seller attraction procedure and training plan.
2. Procedure to prospect.
3. Procedure to identify the needs.
4. Procedure for the presentation.
5. Procedure for closing and answering objections.
6. Customer tracking procedure.
7. Collection procedure.
8. Procedure to request references and testimonies.

How to attract a champion team?

Now that you have a written sales plan and you have your sales procedures, you need to star with the first part of the sales process that is to come up with a champion team of $uper sellers that have the right values, this is the most important part if you have a group and you wish that your company or business increase sales significantly. First make sure that the person has the sales profile you are looking for, you can place psychometric evaluations to ensure that he is the right person in terms of technical and skills as a person or values. Once you have the right team make sure you have a training plan where you make the salespeople all champions, I prefer to train people and sellers than to have someone already made. It's something that I copied to my sports coaches, they preferred to start from scratch with rookie players but they were $uper committed instead of a group of veterans with bad habits and this has given as a result in the case of my coach Nacho Moreno in more than 30 championships in 25 years he has been a sports coach.

"It is **better** to have a **team of rookies** with **few skills**, but with the best attitude and values than to have a team of **veterans** with the **skills**, but very **poor attitude**." David Gaona

5 tools to have a champion team:
1. Have a written common goal.
2. Written code of honor with acknowledgments and consequences.
3. Training plan and strategy in writing and monthly.
4. Daily follow-up and feedback.
5. Well-structured roles and rituals as a team.

You can also read another of my books and audio books called "The 7 keys to form a champion team"
You must have a sales school within your company, and if you are the only seller then you have to make a continuous training plan so that you become a $ super seller. Train with us!
I also need you to understand this, as Henry Ford says:

"The most **expensive** thing is not to **train** your team and they **leave**, but **not to train** them and they **stay** with you forever." Henry Ford

Train your salespeople, train yourself, make your training plan, a $uper Seller is in constant training. You have to understand that everything changes, you're not the same every year, this is why the importance of training monthly, I do it by taking the same trainings every three years- Why? Because it is not the same what I was earning 3 years ago, everything has grown and my solutions have increased, along with my income, then, although in theory the training is the same, I am not, so I see them from a very different perspective. Make a training plan according to your goals, not according to your budget. Train with us!

How to hire a salesperson?

1. Make sure they read and are self-taught.
2. That they are hungry to do more. They must be ambitious.
3. By commissions, pay 20% fixed salary and 80% by results.
4. That has really high energy and good habits like exercising, meditating, etc.

"Make a training plan according to your goals, never according to your budget." David Gaona

Besides investing in having a champion team, giving first class training and training your employees and salespeople, or yourself in case you are independent, you have to invest in acquiring good clients.

What does it mean to buy customers?

Simple, you require to have an advertising or marketing plan, you have to know how you are going to attract your customers, therefore, a list of activities that help you have customers constantly and that they have the need and money to be able to buy your product or service.

"An unmeasured advertisement is an expense, if you measure it and you know how much it costs you to **sell** to each of your clients then it is an **investment**." Philip Kottler

Which is the formula to measure how much does a client cost?

You have to know how much it costs you to attract a new client. It is important to understand and analyze this information all the time because on this should depend what you are going to assign to the sales budget and most importantly you will know what is the most effective way to attract customers to your company.

You need to have the following information.

1. Know where each client comes from, for example, this month we sold 100 products or services to new clients, here it is important that you remove the sales of clients that you already had so that the information is not misinterpreted, 20 were by means of recommendations, 30 were by panoramic announcement, 30 were by the Internet page, 10 by radio announcement and 10 by social networks.
2. You must have the information of how much was sold in total for these 100 customers, this is where you add all the sales, we will assume that you sold 100 thousand dollars with these 100 customers and at the same time know how much was sold by each advertising medium that was proven, for example, by referrals, $ 50,000 was sold, for a panoramic ad, $ 10,000, for a web page, $ 10,000, for a radio ad, $ 20,000, and $ 10,000 for social networks.
3. Now you are going to find out what was the total cost of advertising from the five media that you used, how much the recommendation cost you in this case, we are going to suppose that it cost you a thousand dollars, the cost of the panoramic

advertisement was 10 thousand dollars , the one of the Internet page of 5 thousand dollars, the radio ad 10 thousand dollars and the social networks was 4 thousand dollars, then you define that the total cost was of 30 thousand dollars.

With this information you now have the **IXNC** (Investment per new client), It is it is calculated in a very simple way, the 30 thousand dollars divided among the 100 clients.

IXNC= Publicity Cost/New Clients

IXNC =30,000 dollars/100 new clients = 300 dollars per new client

Now we are going to take the cost for each one of the means of publicity from the example so that you know how you need to make your publicity plan.

IXNC by referrals

IXNC=One thousand dollars/20 new clients = 50 dollars per new client.

IXNC by panoramic ad

IXNC=10,000 dollars/30 new clients = 300 dollars per new client

IXNC by internet page

IXNC=5,000 dollars / 30 new clients = 167 dollars per new client

IXNC by radio announcement

IXNC=10,000 dollars/10 new clients = 1000 dollars per new client

IXNC by social media

IXNC=4,000 dollars/10 new clients = 400 dollars per new client

What do we need those numbers for? So you can have a high efficiency in your sales plan, measure every publicity advertisement, have the data on hand and analyze it.

Advertisement	Attracted Customers	Cost	Sales by this media	IXNC
Referrals	20	$ 1,000	$ 50,000	$ 50
Panoramic ad	30	$ 10,000	$ 10,000	$ 333
Radio	10	$ 10,000	$ 20,000	$ 1,000
Internet page	30	$ 5,000	$ 10,000	$ 167

		$	$	$
Social media	10	4,000	10,000	400

In summary, what I want you to observe is that the investment per new customer for referrals is the lowest and the one that attracts the most sales, with this number you are able to make the decision to invest more to "buy" new clients using both a more aggressive referrals plan and invest more in attracting customers by website.

In contrast, the radio, panoramic ad and social networks are too high according to the average sale per customer. So try and change until you come up with the right advertising formula that works for your business.

Advertisement	Attracted Customers	Cost	Sales by this media	IXNC
Referrals	20	$ 1,000	$ 50,000	$ 50
Panoramic ad	30	$ 10,000	$ 10,000	$ 333
Radio	10	$ 10,000	$ 20,000	$ 1,000
Internet page	30	$ 5,000	$ 10,000	$ 167
Social media	10	$ 4,000	$ 10,000	$ 400

I want to give you an example about the importance of having a measurable publicity plan, a a client that I have since long time ago and has been working in the health industry has more than 20 years being pioneer in this field, they made a not insignificant investment of 40 thousand dollars per month in advertising.

Making the initial evaluation of the return of investment of those 40 thousand dollars, we realized that this money invested monthly was profiting him in attracting 50 clients per month. If you listened well to 50 customers only per month! These clients represented 10 thousand dollars of sales per month. Something unheard of, they had almost 15 years with the same television ad. It is vital to measure each of the advertising means we use to obtain the greatest benefit and above all to know what the return on investment is for each dollar you invest.

So test it, measure every dollar you invest and have a measure of how much it costs you in advertising to attract a new client. An advertising plan must include many aspects you can measure and try a different media, for example:

Website, Facebook, Twitter, You Tube, Google, Radio, Television, flyer, panoramic ads, flyers, door to door, etc. ...

Try everything for a week or two and immediately make the corresponding measurements, make sure that you know how much you receive in sales per every dollar you invest. This is called Guerrilla marketing, make a massive publicity plan and most importantly, measure it. The vital thing in this process is to know how much it costs you to attract a new client. If you need help in this matter we can help you, visit our page www.iexito.com for a personal coaching session or for your company. Train with us!

One of the most important **measurements** as a **$uper Seller** is the average investment to **buy a new client**." Philip Kotler

What language does a $uper seller use?

It is important that you understand that once you have the advertising plan and you execute and evaluate it, month after month the clients will arrive. That is why it is important that you constantly train your salespeople and of course you also continue training.

The vocabulary that we use as $uper sellers is completely different from traditional sellers, remember that purchases are made according to the main function of the brain to approach the pleasure and get away from pain, so I want you to understand that there are certain words that you should constantly use to be able to origin a feeling of pleasure with your clients especially for the creation of trust. Remember that sales are a transfer of emotions of your product or service. The more words you use to cause them greater pleasure the probability of sale is superior.

First we are going to evaluate the words that create pain in the clients and that make the reptilian brain activate, moving the person with whom you are wanting to start a conversation away more and more every time:

Negative Word	Meaning	Positive Word
No	The brain doesn't accept a no, it has heard it for more than 15000 times, so it eliminates it.	Yes
Sale	To be on sale is a synonym of that is left over and that is the last product.	Opportunity
Contract	You will be tied to pay whether you like it or not for the rest of your days for a product or service.	Agreement
Signature	They can use it for fraud.	Ok
Cost	Financially it is related to spending not investing.	Investment
Cheap	Low quality and bad service.	Economic
Lawyer	They are going to get in trouble if	Partner

	they do not like the product or service.	

You are probably going to tell me that some or all of the words that come here described you find a different meaning; sincerely I have to tell you that you are right. But the problem is that you are not in the head of all your clients and you have no idea if the person is thinking what you want to say, they only receive the information and process it so that as a $uper seller you have to understand that You must use the appropriate words or use a set of words that you know will not affect the person you are talking to.

So start to change the words you speak so you can increase your chances of improving your sales, it is that simple. Those words that come up here are some that generally affect the subconscious directly, but don't doubt that you have to find the combination within the head of your customers and know the appropriate words to sell to your client.

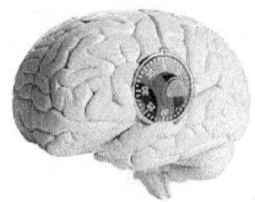

For example, the brain has heard the words "no" or "do not" for more than 30000 times, then by the age of 5 what your brain does is to eliminate it or build a bridge, let's make an exercise close your eyes and I want you to listen to the following:

"Do not think of your mom", "do not think of your mom", "do not think of your mom", "do not think of your mom", "do not think of your mom", "do not think of your mom". In what did you think of?

In your mom logically, I need you to understand that the brain records what you say, but there are words that have another meaning for the other person so you need to use them properly and know when to use them for the benefit of both. It is like if by the right combination of words you are going to unlock the combination of the other person's brain so you can help them.

CIPASA sales system

Now we are going to talk about the *CIPASA* it is important that you memorize the word *CIPASA*, because I want you to realize that if you really use them as a tool you are going to get a satisfactory result or at least I assure higher than what you have been obtaining.

This is not an experiment I need you to comprehend that this tools are 100% proven and we use them in our business and want you to realize that earning money with the *CIPASA* system, that selling more in your business *CIPASA*, that to become a better person and learn how to get along with others *CIPASA*, that you are going to turn into a $uper Seller *CIPASA* so record them in your memory and use them as when you use a spoon to eat, as simple as that. I am going to give you a brief summary so we can later get more into it.

Let's begin with the first letter *C*

Step 1 Contacts with money and pre-qualified

This first step is principal so you can increase the probability of being successful, you have to make sure that each person you contact to offer your product or service has the following two very important characteristics:

1. Has money to be able to buy or at least has the ability to get it.
2. Has the need for your product or service.

In this step, 97% of salespeople fail and that is why frustration increases in the majority and they prefer to give up than to make intelligent effort. Make sure before each visit and before each presentation that the person meets these two characteristics. As hitters in baseball, to improve the percentage of batting you have to improve the technique, remember that sales, as in sports is a matter of statistics, knowing how to filter and finding the right clients will help you increase the probability of closing a sale.

"The quickest way to **lose weight** is trying to sale **without technique** and without pre-qualifying your **clients**." Brian Tracy

Now let's go with letter *I*

step 2 *I*dentifying needs

Learn to ask the right questions to identify the needs of the client, remember that a $uper Seller only speaks 20 to 30%, because the rest of the time we are identifying with accurate questions what is the real need of our client.

The quality of the questions will determine the sale to a large extent because asking correctly will drive the client or buyer to be able to give you information because they know that you are interested, the questions are the success in the sale. Also, as Mr. Maslow says in his research one of the main needs of the human being is to be heard, so this skill will represent many profits, I guarantee it.

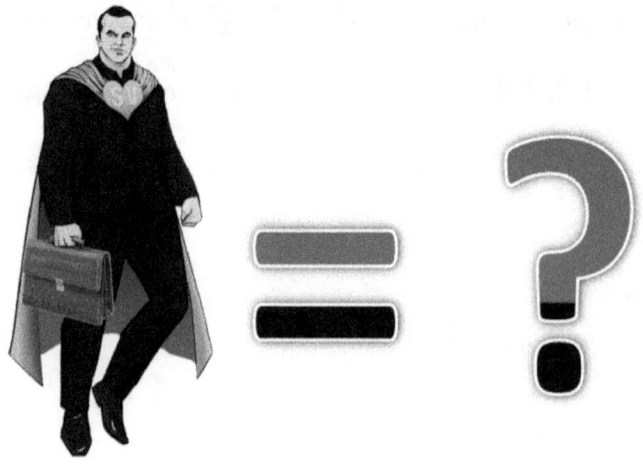

"The quality of the **questions** you make to other **people** and you make to **yourself** determines in great measure the **success** you are going to get."
Tom Hopkins

Now we continue with letter *P*

Step 3 *P*resentation based in needs.

Once you identify your client's need you have to learn to make your presentation versatile, this means that you can adapt it according to what your client needs, you have to find first what is the basic need of our client, also known as the "G-spot" " This spot, is what your client is going to buy is what really moves their reptilian brain, for example, when I sell my productivity company (www.iexito.com) what I have found with our clients is that one of the most attractive benefits is having more free time, so that is one of the main G-spots or benefits that we handle, logically it is not the main one.

Remember that it depends on what your client previously told you. Make sure your presentation is full of your client's basic need or G-spot.

"You have to find your client's G-spot in order to sell to them." David Gaona

Now let's go with letter A

Step 4 Assimilate how to close

You can make an excellent presentation, have the right customer, have identified the G-spot, but if the closures is not your thing, it is as if you love to cook, but you do not like the fire, if you are in sales then you have to learn to enjoy the closures because that's where the biggest advantage is and where the cash register fills up.

There are different closures; here I tell you about several in an acrostic so you can learn them faster.

Close your mouth and sell.

Link your client, get them involved in what you are selling.

Options. Provide several options until you find the right one.

Swing back the question the client has made.

Invincible rhinoceros. Use them as an advisor so they tell you what they need.

Not the right answer and hitching. For example tell them the wrong date so they tell you the right answer of what they want.

Go on. The right moment to be able to sell is when you just finished one.

"The best way to **close** is to **shut up**, make **question**s and sell when your **client asks for it**."

David Gaona

Now we proceed with letter _S_

Step 5 Solicit payment and guarantee of results

The sale is a process and as such you have to understand that you need to learn to request payment and always use the guarantee of results. The best seller is always a satisfied customer, when you have good customers whom you have helped them with your product or service. Always ask them if you can provide them as a reference. It is very rare that any of them will tell you that they will not be able to. Always use your customers as sellers and reward them. Use the guarantee of results and never be ashamed of requesting a payment, remember that your work is worth a lot.

"Selling is a process, requesting payment is part of it so learn to enjoy it." Phillip Kottler

At last we go with letter A

Step 6 Asking for testimonials and referrals (use the wows).

Ask your clients for referrals, if they buy or not make sure they provide information from clients or friends who have the need. Ask them at the end: Can I tell the person you just referred that you recommended them?, using testimonials of your own clients or leveraging is one of the most efficient ways to sell, if possible put a list of your satisfied customers with phones, posts and emails so that people to whom you present them feel more confident that you can contribute.

"**The best seller** within your **company** is the **satisfied client**, learn to **capitalize** them and when you do, **reward them** for it." David Gaona

Evaluate yourself in the CIPASA system

(Place 1 as very low and 5 as expert level)

3. How good are you to obtain contacts with money and with the need?	
4. Do you have a way to generate new contacts constantly?	
5. Do you have a way to identify the client's needs?	
6. Do you have a needs identification questionnaire according to the products or services that you offer?	
7. Do you have different ways to present your products or services according to your client's communication type?	
8. Do you know which is the social style of your clients to be able to present accordingly?	
9. Do you know by heart at least 3 closing strategies?	
10. Do you have identified which are your client's most common objections and the information to answer any concern?	
11. Do you have a written procedure for requesting payment?	
12. Do you have a guarantee of satisfaction for your product or service?	
13. Do you have a list of referrals that your actual clients have provided?	
14. Do you have a plan to benefit those clients who provide referrals?	
15. Do you have a list of testimonials with video, email or something written from your satisfied clients, which you can provide to future clients?	
16. Do you have a written marketing war plan?	
17. Do you have a sales budget assigned per year?	

How did you do in your evaluation?

The importance of being able to measure yourself is that you know where your areas of opportunity are so that you can work on what you most need, to be able to become a $uper Seller and increase your monthly sales income.

In the aspects that you scored high, what you have to do is congratulate yourself, it is important to celebrate every triumph you have, and if you are reading this book I am sure that you are a champion and you already have results and you have been giving them for a long time, but the important thing is not where have you arrived to but where you can get to?

So now what you have to do is a work plan in the aspects you have scored low, you have to work on what you need most, it may be the part of making contacts, closings, the plan of references, in any of them, this evaluation is an X-ray so that you are successful, so make sure you have a cold head for the analysis and make a work plan. Put what you are going to do, who will do it in case it is a work team or company, put a date for when you will finish it and advance percentage. This work plan must be put in writing and daily follow-up to each of the improvement activities for your sales system.

What is the importance of the daily measurement of the entire system?

I want you to understand that this system is infallible if and only if you follow it, now there is a fundamental and absolute part of the CIPASA system and that is that you have to understand that you must measure it daily, you have to make sure that every day you follow your salespeople or in case it's only you, check that you are following the system every day.

The use of indicators is a fundamental part of this system, the indicators is a dashboard that will tell you how you are doing with the sales, whether you are alone or have a company or have people in charge one of the differences of a $uper Seller and one seller from the bunch is that you have daily indicators. The daily follow-up will give you a minimum of 10% more sales in a month, why do I assure you this? Because I have a consulting company, (www.iexito.com) and because every time we help a client to set the daily indicators and follow the minimum system the growth per month is 10%, so I assure you a lot of success if you use the system and you follow it daily, here the key is "Daily", that is right, every day, the meeting must last a maximum of 10 minutes to be able to review all the indicators. If you have any doubt, you can contact us to help you. We are experts in the use of the system and we make companies achieve their goals in record time.

Some examples of daily indicators are:

1. Calls
2. E-mails
3. Sales
4. Quotes
5. New contacts
6. CRM completion

Make your plan, execute it, measure it every day and improve it.

$uper Seller Powers

1. The first thing is that you make an annual sales budget, month by month, what you are going to sell, write the customers, the products and in which areas.
2. Make a training plan for your salespeople, in all steps of the CIPASA sale, in addition to the products or services you offer and make a list of books to start reading.
3. Make a recognition plan for sellers; make sure you only have champions sellers that are the best possible, if necessary 1 or 2 months to choose them.
4. Write 5 achievements that you have had in a goal book, also put your area of recognition in your office or at home.
5. Use your $uper Seller vocabular, make your list of keywords and always use them in any situation remember that this increases your probability of closing and selling.
6. Make a sales evaluation based on the CIPASA system.
7. Learn the CIPASA steps by heart:

a. **C**ontacts with money and pre-qualified

b. **I**dentifying needs

c. **P**resentation based in needs

d. **A**ssimilate how to close

e. **S**olicit payment and guarantee of results

f. **A**sking for testimonials and referrals

POWER =

Information +

Action

Why is it that the first step of the system is having the right contacts for the sale?

Contacts with money
and
prequalification

5

"The fastest way to **lose weight** is trying to sell **without technique** and without prequalifying your **clients**." Brian Tracy

1. Why are sales a matter of probability?

2. Why do people get married?

3. How to make the contact call?

4. Why use CRM?

5. What is the importance of time management?

6. How does a $uper Seller's agenda looks like?

7. $uper Seller Powers

Let's begin with a story: "Once upon a time there was a young man who had the wish to get married so he began looking everywhere and decided to go to a club, which was the place he attended most often, to find the woman of his dreams. Since he was a very determined and obstinate young man he began to ask if they wanted to marry him to each woman sitting in the club, obviously of the 200 women who were in the club, none of them said yes. The very hurt and frustrated young man went to look for a guru to help him understand the situation, the guru replied that he had searched in the wrong place and therefore they were the wrong people.

Let's say that what you do in the **first 2 hours** of the day determines in a **90%** how the **rest of the day** is going to go." David Gaona

This happens very commonly in the world of sales, there are many sellers who have a lot of energy and want to eat the world in 1 month, but they do it without intelligence. Let's talk about the first step of the CIPASA system; the C is to make sure you attract Contacts with money and with the need of your product or service. If you follow these two steps at first you increase the probability of closing by 300%, always keep this in mind so that you can filter with whom you get along to do business or business presentations. It is not that you are a bad person or that you do not want your customers is that as a $uper seller you have to first find the right customers, the ones that really want your product and you don't need to be begging to be bought.

"

"Always keep your **portfolio** full of **potential** clients; always have more **clients** to **visit** than time." Brian Tracy

The identification of needs and presentation is really a mere procedure because if you make sure that your clients look for you instead of your looking for them then the sale becomes much simpler because you do not have to convince them of your products or services. They already want them even before they meet you.

"Even though you are new in the world of sales, you can replace the lack of ability with the quantity of prospects." Jim Rohn

In this first step the time management plays a very important role, because you only have to meet potential clients and this means that they have the money and the need or at least if you are going to see them is because they will give you references . In your agenda make sure that your potential referenced clients (these are those that your satisfied customers are recommending to you), are the ones that you give preference to be able to present to, make the call or send them the information.

"Remember that your **referred potential clients** go **first** in your **agenda** to be able to sell to them." David Gaona

Did you know that sales are a matter of probability?

Sales are a number game, you have to improve your likelihood of being able to sell with the first step of the CIPASA system having the proper contacts, this is the first step, this increases the probability of closing, as long as you do not have very clear to whom you should sell and especially if they have the need is complicated to do something.

The better prospects you have the better you will do, then you have to think about the following questions:

How do I do it to attract better clients?

What places should I frequent to have better prospects?

Are the clients that I currently have are recommending me?

How can I satisfy my clients' needs in a better way?

The quality of the questions you ask will improve your results. Remember that sales are a matter of probability, measure them, I want you to become crazy for sales, in an analytical without falling into paralysis by analysis, which is when you have so many numbers you do not know where to turn or what to do with the numbers.

Why do people get married?

The answers you can give me are for love, money, need, for not staying alone, etc. ... But none of these is correct, the main reason why people get married is because they put a date, so I want you to do a plan of 500 referrals, put a date when you are going to contact them, make a list of 500 people you know, you have to think about all the people you can present your products or services, although this does not mean that you are going to do it because you have to make sure that these customers have the need and the money but at least you have to have the list ready, the next step is that you have to segment them, for example put a number 1, to those contacts of yours who have the need and the money to be able to obtain your product or service.

If you notice it is really easy to make your list of contacts, follow these 3 simple steps:

1. Make your list of potential contacts.
2. Classify your contacts by contact priority.
3. Set the date when you will contact them.

Now once you have found the clients within your contacts with the need and the money, then what you have to do is start talking to them. At the beginning 80% of your time is going to be spent making phone calls to be able to make appointments and then after a several time you will have more appointments than calls, just make sure you make at least 10 calls a day, for this you have to do very well in managing your time and those calls make them between appointments or even have someone who is making contacts for you.

"Let's say that the most **appropriate person** to leave a task to is the one that is **most occupied** all the time." David Gaona

What is the objective of the contact call?

The contact call must be a call not to sell, but to make the appointment. Unless the client wants to buy immediately, but remember that the first thing you want to do is build trust with the customer. If you are a person that you already know and have a friendship with, then you have to talk to say hello and to make the appointment. If you are a person you do not know then you can ask a direct question like the following:

Would you like to know a proven method to increase productivity by 30%?

If the answer is affirmative then, you give a little more information on the phone, but only enough to leave them interested in the next appointment. Remember that the call is to be able to maintain or reestablish contact, it might take you a couple of weeks to schedule an appointment and about 10 phone calls, remember that the first thing you are doing before selling is establishing a trust between the person and you.

The first appointment is not for sale, turn off the cell phone and pay as much attention as possible. Keep in mind that it will take you at least 5 appointments to sell, so be patient and take your repertoire of questions to know where you can meet their needs.

Which are the keys to sell in a phone call?

1. Mention their name at least 10 times on the call.

2. Have them tell you at least 10 times "yes" with questions. Eg, do you know Carlos Ramírez? Are you Miguel Hernández? Carlos talked to you about one of the workshops?

3. Put a mirror in front of you so you always smile.

4. Very good energy.

5. Use testimonials from people who have achieved results. We have had people who after 3 months earn 100% more; the achievements are depending on the workshop.

6. Ask closing questions at the end: Do you want to enter the PSL or PCM workshop? For one or 2 people? With credit card or deposit?

7. Always seek to close the sale at the end.

8. Tie the payment.

9. Investigate their needs with questions.

10. Sell them the information according to their needs.

Categorize your clients, Customer type a, type b, type c, type a are the clients who have the money and who have the need, type b are clients who have the need or money, and type c, have no money neither the need, but they can be a source to give you prospects, so devote yourself to make good relations with the people around you to make a very good list of prospects. Train with us!

What is the CRM?

Customer Relationship Management is a term of the information industry that applies to methodologies, software and, in general, Internet capabilities that help a company to manage relationships with its customers in an organized manner. For example, a company could create a customer database that describes the relationships in sufficient detail so that management, sales agents, service workers, and, perhaps, customers, can directly access that information, respond to the needs of customers with product plans and offers, remind customers of different service needs, know what other products a customer has purchased, and so on.

The use of this tool is very important to be able to save contacts, number of visits, calls, quotes, etc. ...

Everything that has to do with customers can be downloaded in this tool, I highly recommend that you work with it to be able to speed things up, make your list of your 500 contacts there so that you can more efficiently manage the information. There are many options in the market for a very affordable price.

Now the question I am going to ask you is very important. Where do the main clients come from? This is an example of a Latin American service company serving all over the world, of more than 5000 clients around the world:

• 75% come from referrals from the same clients.
• 10% of the internet page.

- 10% cold contact.
- 15% of others.

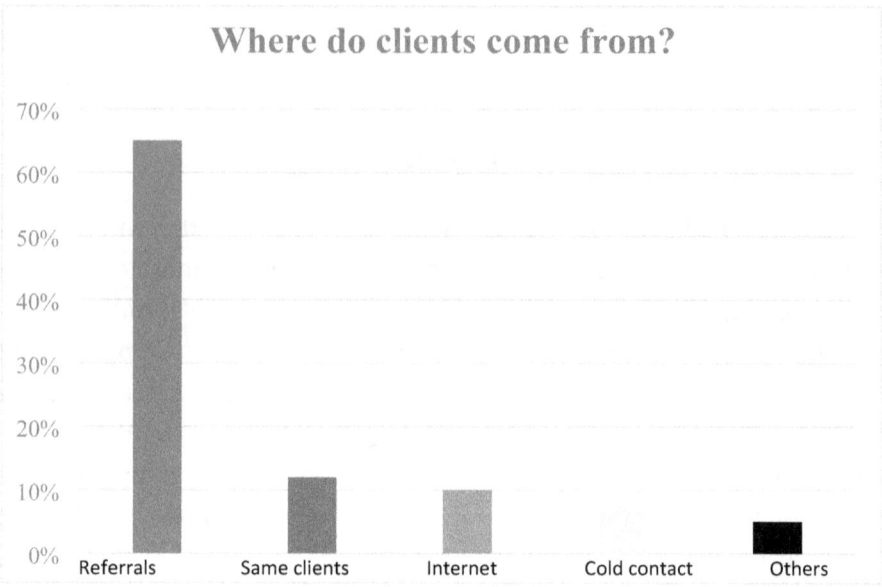

Where do clients come from?

This is why it is important to have good referrals and manage the customer database as well as possible, keep in mind that this will be the main source of income for your business for many years if you manage it properly.

What is the importance of time management?

Keep in mind that as a $uper Seller you must manage your time as your best treasure, every minute is worth gold and many dollars so learn to be as efficient as possible.

You have to start filtering the activities that generate you value and those that do not generate it, just as you have to learn to separate contacts that generate you money and those that do not generate it. That's why we're going to talk about time management.

"I only **eat, think, talk, take and do** stuff that take me to my **goals**." David Gaona

Stephen Covey describes a model of 4 Quadrants to manage time.

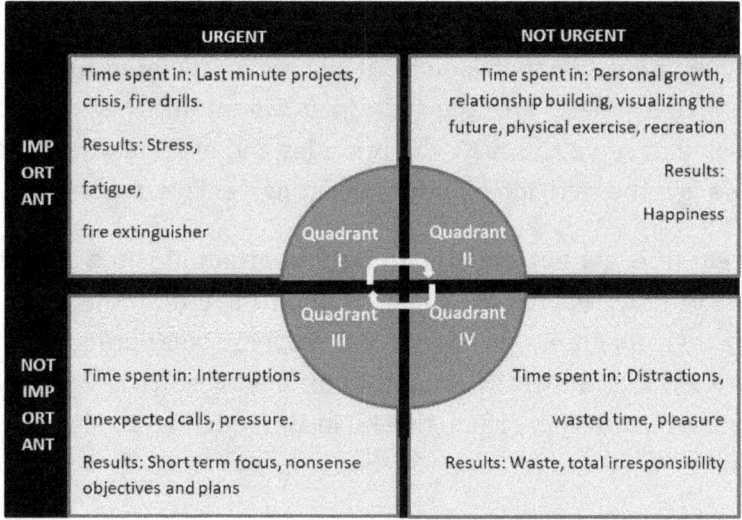

Quadrant I is about what's important and urgent, it is in which we move every day, where we produce, apply our experience. These are issues that demand our immediate attention. Some activities are important, but we have been postponing them so much, or we have not planned them enough, that they have already become urgent, thus a crisis arises. These are pressing problems, projects with deadlines, meetings, the more we focus on this quadrant, the more it dominates us and leaves us less room for maneuver. It is the quadrant of stress and exhaustion.

Quadrant II the important but not urgent, the quadrant of quality, where we plan in the long term, anticipate and prevent problems, increase our skills and provide us with continuous development. In it we invest in listening and in our relationships with others, allowing us to increase our execution capabilities. It is the quadrant of personal leadership, of foresight and preparation: we act on it. It gives us the power to generate capacity.

Quadrant III is the urgent but not important, the quadrant of deception. Here we spend most of our time (sometimes mistakenly believing that these are activities in quadrant I). They are usually activities that serve to satisfy the priorities and expectations of others. Here we find the calls, interruptions, meetings, emails, reports.

Quadrant IV is the not urgent and not important, it is the quadrant of the loss of time, where we usually escape to flee from the overwhelm caused by quadrants I and III. It implies deterioration without consistency; it is not worth or contributes anything: trivial tasks such as spam mail, advertising, coffee, breaks, inconsequential conversations.

After reflecting on this matrix, it is time to ask some questions:

- Where did you spend most of your time last week? In what quadrant?

- What important things did not receive your time and attention?

- What is the activity that you know that if you performed it with excellence and without rest it would have resulted in important positive results in your personal / professional life?

- And if you know all this, why do not you do it?

Because they are not urgent or pressing. They do not act on you, you are the one who has to act on them.

The difference between what is urgent and what is important

In productivity, much has already been written about how to treat each type. However, it is quite useless to explain how you should act with the tasks of these two classes if we do not know how to classify them to begin with. Mea culpa and a thousand thanks for the warning.

Actually, it's not such a complicated thing, but if we want to do it almost instantaneously so as not to flood our task lists with completely useless things, let's start at the beginning.

Definitions

Do not tell battles, the difference is easy and if you doubt in some cases, however rare they may be, you may not have the concept completely clear. That is why we go to the definitions that are the basic pillar of all reasoning.

Urgent task

It is a quality associated with time. It increases both as you have less time left for the deadline, and with the size of the task.

• If two tasks take the same time to do them, the most urgent is the one that has the closest deadline.

• If two tasks have the same deadline, the most urgent one is the one that takes the most time.

• If the deadline for a task is postponed, it becomes less urgent.

• If you discover that a task will be longer than you thought, it will become more urgent.

• A task that has no deadline, will never be urgent.

As you see, the language does not help much. In fact, when we say that a task is urgent, what we mean is that it is "very urgent", whereas when we say that a task is not urgent, we should really say that it is "not very urgent". From the moment you have a deadline, a task is at least a little bit urgent.

Important task

It is a quality associated with the consequences. A task increases its importance if the consequences of failing in it increase. In other words, a task is important only if the consequences we will suffer by not doing it are serious.

• Two tasks, regardless of the volume of work or difficulty, with similar consequences, are equally important. (Example: as important is writing a report as taking it to the right person)

• Of two tasks, although not at all similar, the most important will always be the one that causes the most serious effects in case of not completing it.

• Even if the task does not change, the consequences may change. If they do, the importance of the task changes (increases or decreases).

How to differentiate an urgent task from an important one?

If you have understood the above correctly, you will see that this very common question does not make sense. The importance and urgency of a task are attributes. Just as a person can be smart and short at the same time, a task can be urgent and important at the same time.

Also, this is not black or white, it has a whole gray scale. In one axis you have the urgency of the task and in another you have the importance.

How to measure urgency?

I'm going to give you the measure I use to organize tasks from most to least urgent. As I explained before, a task is more urgent if it is longer and the less time is left to do it.

From this it can be deduced that the least urgent task possible is one that is done instantaneously (0 seconds) or for which you have infinite time (what in the real world means: there is no deadline).

With this in mind, this is my measure of urgency:

$$\text{Urgency} = \frac{\text{time it takes to complete the task}}{\text{remaining time until deadline}}$$

From this we deduce that all the tasks will be between 0 and 1 meaning:

• 0: It is not urgent nor will it ever be

• 1: You must dedicate absolutely all your time to that task or you will not get it done before the deadline

Finally, some of us may ask: But what if I feel that the urgency is more than 1? That would mean that the time the task takes you is more than the time you have left. As it is evident, it is already an impossible task.

Do not waste efforts starting something that will not give results, or, on the contrary, negotiate to extend the deadline.

And the importance?

The importance is extremely subjective, it depends absolutely on you. There is no homogeneous measure.

I know that this conclusion may sound a little frustrating, but in reality it is, on the contrary, I recommend that you protect this constantly. If someone changes the importance you give to each task, it could indirectly control what you do.

Your mother when she wanted you to eat a plate of lentils threatened to leave you without going out to play. In our model, that is neither more nor less than changing the context. The consequence of staying hungry was the addition of not being able to play later. Therefore, you ended up perceiving the task as more important. It's scary seen like that, huh? Fortunately, our mothers did it because lentils have a lot of iron!

That is why I say that not only do I give you a method to order the importance, but I encourage you to be the one who defines it exclusively.

"In the **business world**, we all have **24 hours**, whether you earn a thousand dollars or **1 million dollars per hour**, the difference is in what you occupy your time and how do you administer it." David Gaona

So please use your time wisely, as $uper Seller you have to spend most of your time with clients that generate more or may generate profit, be very selfish in this regard and focus on just spending time in presentations or doing contacts that generate more sales or make you a better seller or person.

How does a $uper Seller's agenda should look like?

First of all, the $uper Seller must always manage an agenda. On Sundays you must make the agenda of the whole week, do not focus on meeting the agenda 100% remember that everything has changes, in fact, what happens to me is that I meet my agenda about 50% but I focus on doing what is more important but not so urgent for my business, family and for my body.

After I make my weekly schedule, every day at night I check that I complied and planned the next day of my activities. As a $uper Seller you have to work in all the steps of the sale, you have to assign time in your schedule to make contacts, to make presentations, to make quotes, to make collections, to request referrals, recognition calls, exercise, meditations , family visits, etc.

It is important for your daily life that you have your family within your agenda, you need to have something besides work, also activities like exercise, reading, meditation. Keep in your agenda all of these things, if you have it in your agenda I assure you that your habits will improve. At the beginning it will seem complicated, but you will realize that in a period of time you will get used to it, but then again remember it is important that you assign time in your agenda.

Why do you have to be making calls 80% of the time?

The important thing is that at the beginning you focus on the 10 hours that you work, 8 hours are destined to make calls so that there comes a time when you have so many appointments and presentations that you only dedicate 10 or 20% of your time, but first focus on doing 40 to 50 calls daily, this is the key, you have to make 1 call every 5 minutes minimum. This is what we do as $uper Sellers, one of the things that I remember most of a course I took with Mr. Dan Peña is that he says that the key to being a billionaire is that you make 100 calls a day to offer your product and make sure that every salesperson in your organization does the same.

Why is it important to become friends with the receptionist?

Since you make your calls I want you to understand one thing, the fact that you get along well with the receptionist or the person at the entrance of the company you are going to visit is that they can give you a lot of information about whether or not your client is available, this has always helped me to secure my appointments, learn the name and bring very simple gifts to them on their birthday, give small gifts so that you have them on your side, if you have them as an ally they will become your seller within the organization because they know who or when your clients are inside the company.

What are the 5 steps to cold prospecting?

1. **Visit places where you may find clients with money or need.** Please make an analysis of where the potential customers are or where they

are going, what you can do is do a study with your current clients and ask them where they spend their free time.

2. **Make a list of mirror-like questions to be able to establish a conversation.** These questions are the entrance, you never arrive presenting yourself with someone you do not know, you have to arrive asking questions about the activity they are doing, it is also important that you know how to read the right moment to get to ask the questions when the person is available to do it.

1. How are you?
2. It is cold outside right?
3. Did you decorate your office yourself?
4. Is this desk really wood?
5. Do you like to read?
6. Is the food of this restaurant appetizing?
7. Do you like to come to the park?
8. Do you like to exercise?
9. Are you from Mexico?
10. Do you like watching movies?

3. **Discuss what interests them.** Once you ask the questions, then any clue they give you or information they provide use it to keep talking about what they are talking about, if you see them reading then ask them Do you like to read?, and ask the name of the book then you have to ask them more about the information that they have just given you about books.

4. **Help them in their business selflessly.** Since you have entered and after about 10 minutes of hobby talk then you enter in the subject, but you have to make sure that you first introduce yourself and then ask them what they do and see how to help them first, remember first you have to plant remember it.

5. **After helping them ask for references or introduce them to the business.** Once you have given them references or helped in some way in their business then you tell them what you do and that you can help them with, in case they tell you they do not require your product or service, then you ask for references from someone that they know that might be interested.

"If you **focus** on activities like searching for **prospects, presenting,** and giving follow-up to **clients,** then sales will come by themselves." Brian Tracy

What are the 7 mistakes of Prospecting in cold?

1. **Presenting the product or service since the beginning.** Approaching and presenting to every person you encounter, will make many people in the network marketing business turn the other way from you.
2. **Yearning to sale since the beginning.** Thinking the sale with be achieved from the beginning, before generating any confidence.
3. **Interrupting a conversation to get in.** Stop observing the surroundings and interrupting people when they're talking, especially when we don't know them.
4. **If they're eating or in interrupting while having an important chat.** While they're eating, it's very uncomfortable when somebody offers you something and they know you're doing something else.
5. **Approaching the wrong person.** Approaching somebody that doesn't fit the profile by not imagining or reading the person right, you end up wasting your time.

6. **Going to the wrong place.** There's times and places, you need to learn there's some places where you don't prospect, even though this doesn't happen 100% of the times.
7. **Start without asking questions.** Start presenting or offering your product or service is a terrible mistake as the person doesn't know you yet.

Phone call example with someone you know

$uper Seller: Hello client. How are you? How's everything going?

Client: Excellent, really good actually. How about you?

$uper Seller: Excellent client, always improving, sales are growing and I'm training. To tell you the truth, I'm really happy. I have sold 40% more than before and I'm doing really well with my family. (He mentions all the benefits he's had with his training). Truthfully, I'm really happy with the things I've been learning. (Get his interest in the training).

Client: Oh great! It's wonderful to hear that. What are you doing so things work out for you?

$uper Seller: Client, let me just say that the trainings I'm taking are really great, especially one called Unlimited Power given by a Mexican coach in 4 different countries, that has changed my life and millions of people's too. They taught me how to structure goals, how to walk on glass (You get into more detail of everything that happens there). I have friends that earn twice as much now, people that have opened their business, another friend doubled their sales. etc.

Client: Sounds really interesting. So, where did you take it? When was it?

$uper Seller: Now that you ask, let me tell you we're bringing it to Miami as our objective is to help more people and businessmen get the same benefit we did. He will come xxxx date to Miami. Are you interested in getting the same results we did?

Client: Yes, of course.

$uper Seller: Oh good! How many people would you like to invite?

Client: I'd like to go with my wife.

$uper Seller: Perfect! Two spots then, look, the investment is $350 USD each, but I'll give them to you both for $500 USD. Would you like to pay with credit card or cash?

Client: Credit Card is fine.

$uper Seller: Visa or Master Card?

Client: Visa is fine.

$uper Seller: Please give me the numbers on your card and the expiration date.

Client: 491526153419 and expiration date 02-20.

$uper Seller: Excellent, thank you very much! I´ll send you with all the information of the place and what you need to take right away. Can you please give me your email?

Client: Sure, my email is client@hotmail.com.

$uper Client: Thank you very much client! I promise it will change your life. Can you please give the phone numbers of 5 people we could help in your business that could go to the training?

Client: Yes, here they are, client 1(123123123123...), client 2...

$uper Client: Thank you so much for your time client, we'll wait for you in the training.

Client: Excellent $uper Seller, I'll see you there.

$uper Seller Powers

1. Make your 500 people list so you can prospect and segment them with: number 1, the ones with high priority, and number 2, the ones you need to contact as second priority, that at least have the need or the money.
2. Enlist the activities you do during the day and get rid of the ones with no value or that don't generate any benefit to your business, personal life, health, or any of your goals.
3. Do your complete weekly schedule Sunday afternoon and revise it, daily.
4. Check your agenda every day before 6 am, stablish 5 daily priorities for yourself, and don't go to bed before you finish them. Be disciplined in fulfilling those five things.
5. Personal mirror questionnaire to prospect in cold.

6. Search for places, associations, Chambers of Commerce, or establishments where you can find your clients.
7. Look for having at least from 15 to 20 daily contacts, preferably, recommended.

Power = Information + Action

Why do you have to make questions before any sale?

Identifying Needs

6

"The quality of the questions you ask to other people and to yourself, will determine the level of success you will obtain." Tom Hopkins

1.   Why do you have to memorize names?
2.   What's important about the questions?
3.   What are the 7 questions needed to find the emotion?
4.   What do you need to ask in order to find the G Point?
5.   Who is the best Seller?

6. What's the art of listening and finding the G Point?

7. $uper Seller Powers

How to have chemistry with your client?

Your client is a person who has feelings, it doesn't matter if he's a CEO or a company owner, and they feel. The first thing you need to do as a $uper Seller is to learn how to read their feelings. It's vital you please understand the way you treat your client will be the way he treats you, so treat them as if they were the most important people. You have to fill out a list of requirements in order to be able to listen to a person as if they were the most important people in the world, so the other person feel like they are the most important ones. Before you go to an appointment with you client, you have to follow these 11 steps:

1. Research about his company or person before visiting them, know their history and confirm the appointment 1 hour prior.
2. Have 0 distractions; make sure to turn off our cell phone before the appointment starts.
3. Take a notebook with you in order to take notes about everything they say.
4. Memorize their names and their family's names.
5. If you struggle with their name then write it down the notebook.
6. When you're talking with your client make sure you're right in front of him.
7. Imitate their movements.

8. Scan everything going around them so you can know what to ask them about.
9. Identify their hobbies so you know what to talk to them about.
10. He needs to talk 80% of the time, 20% of it, you make him questions.
11. Prepare and make sure to have the right questions in order to find their G Point.

"A **sale** is done during the **first 60 seconds** in which you meet a **person**." Tom Hopkins

What is the importance of learning the names by memory?

The sale takes place in the first 60 seconds you spend with the client, for you to learn their names by memory is one of the keys, one of the basic needs of a human being is to be heard and the most beautiful word they can hear coming out of your mouth is their name.

So learn their names by heart, once they tell it to you repeat it 30 times and write it in your note pad, you may use mnemonics technique to learn them.

The first step of learning is having interest, recognizing that the topic is important to us or will bring benefit to our lives. Without this element, any observation technique will have no sense.

To facilitate the memorization of proper names is convenient to give them some sense, assign an image. When they are abstract, you need to attach them concrete representations. By general rule, the transformation from the abstract to concrete makes memorization easier.

The strategy that facilitates the retention of proper names consists in assigning, to those names, several mental images.

CREATIVE OBSERVATION: One face with one name

If we want to relate one face to one name, we will use the creative observation technique.

Examples:

1. A client we've just met is named Reynoso. We imagine him with a crown over his head (rey means king in Spanish) and a crossed out bear (oso means bear in Spanish): rey no oso: Reynoso.
2. For someone called Vazquez, we could see his face in a basketball hoop.

Another strategy: IMAGE ASSOCIATION

Pick a facial feature from the person whose name you want to memorize. Maybe their eyes, nose, ears, hair can draw our attention...

To this facial feature we need to assign an image, stablish an association of ideas or creating a verbal codification, phonetics or any other type.

It can also call our attention the physical features of a person, their way of walking, their look, or a feature of their character, or they may suggest kindness, sadness, anger, sweetness; or mayby they can remind us of someone else for their resemblance.

To summarize, it is ALWAYS possible to stablish an association of ideas, images or words.

So learn your client's name by heart. The first 60 seconds you spend with your client will determine 80% of the probability of closing the sale.

"The sale of your **product** or **service** is obtained in the **first** and **last 60 seconds.**" Tom Hopkins

Which are the 5 steps to cause a good impression in the first 60 seconds?

1. **Clothing.** Please dress according to your client, you have to mimic with them, you always have to be at the level of clothing they are wearing, if you go to a manufacturing company avoid wearing a suit, wear what the common denominator of the people wear. Use colors like black, blue and white.

2. **Call them by their name and use proper vocabulary.** Have on hand a list of proper words to use for the sale, remember to talk with the adequate words and to also have versatility to change the way according to the cultural level of your client. If you are talking to a kid is very different as if you are talking to the company's owner or to a housewife, what it's a common denominator is to always call them by their name.

3. **The greeting.** The first words shouldn't be strong, just a "Hi Carlos, mi name is David Gaona." The handshake should be firm but without being too tight, unless the other person squeezes you then you just return the squeeze, but never hurting the other person. Say at least 5 times their name in the first 60 seconds.

4. **The first question.** This has to be something that you have perceived, it can be a How are you? It is really hot outside! How is the company doing?, depends on what you observe around you.

5. **The scanning.** This 15 second scan should give you enough information to be able to know the next questions you are going to ask, observe how the person is doing emotionally, observe the photographs, their desk, the people around, the books on their shelves, observe and begin working in the next questions.

Now that those crucial 60 seconds have gone by, then find out about their emotional state before you begin, ask question so you can find out if they are in the right moment, a $uper Seller knows which is the right time for the sale, there are times when you are simply not going to sell to the client or the person you are with, so this is the time when you sit down and really show interest for them, see how you can help, let them know you are not going to sell, that you are just there to help and if the sell takes place will be in other occasion.

Why should you ask a lot of questions?

Ask the following questions to get to know their mood:

How are you?

How's the family?

How are you doing at school?

How are your parents?

You have to ask targeted questions depending on how you see the mood, the scan you made the first minutes you have been in the office or meeting place, it is valid to ask questions of the situation that is currently happening but keep it very simple.

If you notice that your client wants to keep talking about the topic then you must keep asking them questions about the same topic, for example, if they are angry ask the following question:

Are you angry?

To which they will answer yes, and the next question you are going to ask is Why?, then for sure they are going to answer that one of their children or employees do not obey them and that they have a lot of workload, so you keep asking questions about the same topic until they feel relief or you find the right time or what I call G-POINT, which is the most basic need that the person will want to satisfy immediately.

Which are the 7 questions to find out a person's mood?

1. Are you angry?
2. Do you feel upset?
3. Are you sad?
4. Do you feel gloomy?
5. Why do you feel pensive?
6. Are you happy?
7. Are you excited?

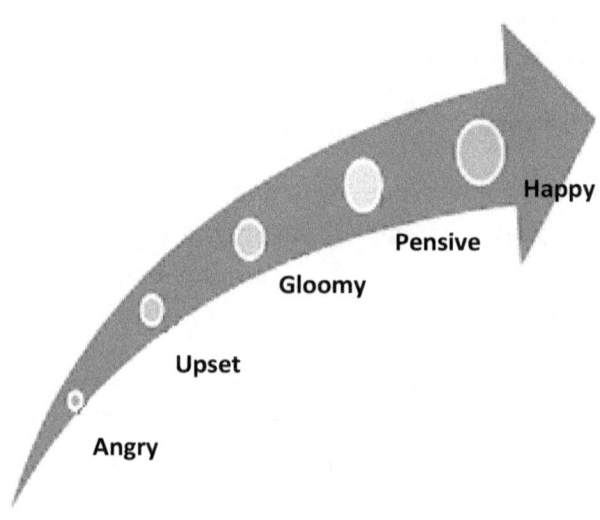

Once you find the G-SPOT, then you need to keep asking question of that fundamental need. There is where you begin digging in the topic before you start selling your product or service.

Which questions do you need to ask to find your client's G-SPOT or basic need?

Now that you know that the child or the employee is your client's main difficulty that your client wants to solve then you begin asking and digging on that topic, these are some questions you may ask:

So your child is having trouble at school? or So your employee has been arriving late to work?, Only this employee or some others?, at the beginning it may appear a little bit mechanic, but you are really going to find out that asking questions is like a muscle, you need to ask the right questions to truly connect with the person, use the Pareto rule, let your client talk the 80% of the time and you only talk 20%, at the beginning if you feel uncomfortable which is most likely if you are not used to asking questions, do it mechanically, ask questions and then shut up.

The 11 mirror questions:

1. How are you?
2. It is cold outside right?
3. Did you decorate your office yourself?
4. Is this desk real wood?
5. Do you like to read?
6. The food in here is really tasty right?
7. Do you like to come to the park often?
8. Do you like to work out?
9. Are you from Mexico?
10. Do you like watching movies?
11. Do you speak English?

What you say is not what sells; if possible try not to make affirmations about your product or service, it is better to ask a lot of questions." Brian Tracy

I will recommend that you practice asking questions, make a sales club where you invite 5 or 6 salespeople from the same or other business and practice with them asking questions, make your meetings as the knights of the round table did them, use your friends to practice asking questions and identifying the G-SPOT.

Who is the best salesperson?

I want to tell you an anecdote of the thousands that have occurred to me with the use of the asking questions tool, about 10 years more or less when I was working in a multilevel company (the best sales school there is), I had to give a presentation in front of 10 people and there was an old lady about 60 years old that never let anyone speak so everybody rejected her, she was one of my associates guests, and I as a leader and $uper seller has to work with her the closings, she had a lot of questions and needed to talk to me.

So I applied the Shut up and listen!, I sat with her for a full hour, first she told me about her health problems, they had detected her cancer, her husband had left her, her children didn't talk to her, she had no job, she had no dreams, and the principal thing she told me is that nobody listened to her. So she began crying, she told me that nobody had sat with her and in many years nobody had listened with that much attention as I had done it. That she thanked me for everything I did, that I was an angel, the creator had sent me to her, that I had changed her life. The only thing I did was to LISTEN.

I only asked sincere questions about what was occurring and got interested for her. At the end she told me she would join the business, that at any business I was into she would join. At that moment she joined and became one of my main leaders at that time and for many years.

"Just shut up and **listen**!" David Gaona

I didn't gave her therapy, nor tools, nor medicine, nor advice, nor hugs, nor money, I just sat with her and listened, I got interested without prejudice, without joining anyone's side, just listen and pay attention to their words, this is what us $uper Sellers do, we just listen, we just interest in others, listening is an art do it with your heart.

How to sell without selling?

You need to know how to listen.

Many not so pleasant situations of daily life, of relationships, in our work, with friends and in general could be avoided if we only knew how to listen better. Listen to others as much as to listen our internal voice. Isn't it true? Because most of the time we are submerged in our daily routine , thinking about everything and nothing at the same time, we omit paying attention to what happens around us, to what others are telling us, we just let go on auto pilot.

It is proven that the majority of people listen to only 25% of what others are saying. A frequent practice is to listen only to the words and not to the feelings expressed or the intention of those words. Even, before a person finished talking, generally, we already have an answer, surpassing and not letting the other person express completely their feelings or needs.

This is because people have already made a decision before listening to arguments. the have a prejudice about what they are going to tell them; they have expectations about what they want to be told; they lack concentration, they lose interest, there is noise in the environment or in their mind, they have a lot of pressure.

We lack the habit of understanding that selling is listening to needs the other person has, to pay attention and to be in their shoes to understand from their perspective, what is it that they need or what is best for that person who is communicating a wish, a desire, a need, an unsolved situation. It is necessary to be selfless and not to think only about ourselves. They say that the best way to get ahead is by giving each other a hand and that if you want to forget about your problems, you need to dedicate yourself to be useful to others.

"**Never criticize**, condemn or **complain** during a **conversation** with a **client** or a prospect."
Brian Tracy

Next, I will share some advice and techniques that the self-development specialist before mentioned offers. I suggest you apply these steps not only to actively listen to others, not only to sell, but to listen to yourself when you have to solve or meditate about an important decision or step in your life.

What do you need to do to actively listen?

1. **Pay a lot of attention:** Stop what you are doing. Don't speak; keep your hands away from your phone, put the pen aside. Keep listening, even if the person sounds wrong or irrelevant.

2. **Relax and let the other person relax too:** If you accomplish that your interlocutor feels relaxed, you are half way there. It will help them say better what they came to say. Do not use your authority on them.

3. **Use body language:** Express interest in what the other person is saying, nodding, smiling or similar gestures.

4. **Do not interrupt:** Listen carefully without interrupting. In this way, the person is going to feel that they have somebody they can trust and they will reveal their true feelings.

5. **Show sympathy:** Make it clear that you are interested on them. Ask your interlocutor to help you understand the problem.

6. **Repeat what they told you:** Make it until your interlocutor tells you "yes, exactly". Paraphrasing clarifies the meaning and helps understanding.

7. **Don't fear the silence:** Silence let's reflect about what the other person has said. Even if it seems uncomfortable, you should not fear it.

8. **Focus in the problem not in the behavior:** Emotions may twist any situation.

9. **Answer:** At least say "I understand". (There are other techniques below)

10. **Express your feelings:** Tell them what you feel, but not before understanding how the other person feels. Although, you should not get emotionally involved in the situation.

11. **Pay attention to the attitude:** Any gesture, mood or topics they evade may be the key about what they are really trying to say.

And these 4 techniques, key steps, to help the other person get talking:

1. **Stimulate:** Show interest to accomplish that the other person keeps talking. Answer "I understand...", "I see ...", "Aha ...", or "That is interesting".

2. **Reformulate:** Show that you are listening and understanding. Repeat what the other person said, emphasizing in the facts.

Say things like " I understand correctly, your idea is …" or "in other words…".

3. **Reflect:** Show that you understand what the other person feels. Answer "you are feeling that …" or "that has you upset".

4. **Summarize:** Make a brief summary of the most important facts, emphasizing on the progress up to that moment, and stablishing the bases to keep talking. Say things like "to summarize…".

Once you learn to listen and you make sure to find your client's, partner's, friend's G-SPOT. Then you need to come back to questioning. The most simple but most effective are the ECO questions, where you need to ask exactly the last sentence they just told you, it is a really obvious question, but it will keep you and your client hooked in the conversation.

The first appointment must be to identify needs, you need to train yourself so that in your first appointment you just listen, it is about making the right questions to assure a next appointment to present, that makes you look professional, there are some occasions where you are going to be able to present your product on the same day and it also depends on your business.

It will also depend on the experience you gain, if you have your presentation ready with time ahead, it may happen that you have done already a lot of presentations and depending on the need you already have the one that meets that need, it is also valid, but then you need to know that the first part of the appointment is going to be to find the G-SPOT before presenting, if they gave you an appointment for an hour then the first 30 or 40 minutes are going to be to identify the basic need to which you are going to orient your presentation.

At which point do you need to understand that you should not sell?

1. If the person is mad or upset, if you just saw they had a discussion or is arguing with someone at that moment.
2. If you heard him answering a call about a problem with someone.
3. If you see them sad or crying.

I want you to understand that not selling at that moment means selling at another time, you need to learn to read situations, you need to make a simple analysis as a $uper Seller and if the person at that moment has a negative mood and you want to sell them anyways; the person is going to relate your product or service with a negative feeling. Please understand that in negative moments for your client the best thing to do is to listen and ask them a lot of questions for them to vent.

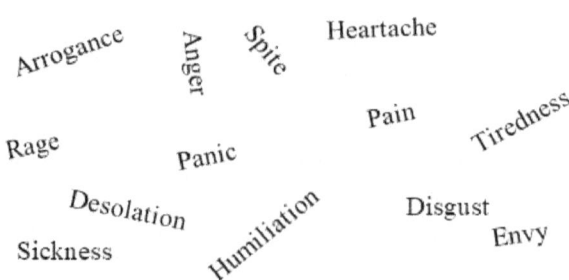

With this am I saying you should not sell?

It depends on the situation if your product or service is going to help them radically with that particular situation then yes, but without pressuring and without using technique. But if your product or service doesn't influence that situation directly, then do not sell. I know that at the time is complicated but you need to understand that the brain works on pain and pleasure and if you sell in an emotionally critical time what their brain is going to do is to relate your products or services with that painful sensation.

Please learn how not to sale, for its also a part of the process of turning you into a $uper Seller. This helps relations to become long term and that such clients recommend you with other clients.

If you see them crying or being angry about something, you have to understand this is not the proper moment. Believe me, the first thing they'll think if you tell them not to talk about their product, business, or service is that you really care for them.

"**Not selling** to your client if they're facing a difficult moment, **means** to make for yourself a lifetime client in another time." David Gaona

Sensing Positive Emotions During a Sale

Now, let's suppose it's the other side of the coin for your client talking about feelings. You caught them earning more money, or laughing, they just had a call where they managed to close a deal, their son called them to say he was doing great in school. So, this is a great indicator for you to use the necessities questionnaire to determine what to sell them. Sensing the right emotion of the sale is an art in the making and your main skill as a $uper Seller.

¿What are the positive emotions in a sale?

Hu
mb
len
ess

Pri
de

Rejocing

Love   Ect
       as
       y

En
th
usi

Optism

Friendship

Eu
ph
ori

Glee

Joy

Pleassure

Ser
eni
ty

Affection

Pleasantness

Ask them about their hobbies. If you already know they love playing football, then you have to talk about it, deepen the subject. If you have a one-hour appointment with them, then you talk about their hobbies with them for 15 times, in this case, football is good. You have to learn to talk about any subject, remember you don´t need to know everything about everything, you just have to make the right questions.

What´s the G Point?

The right set of questions would be like what´s your favorite football team? How they do this weekend? Do you go to watch their games at the stadium? How´s your team doing during the championship games? Deepen in to it, you have to make his subconscious brain feel pleasant when he talks to you and that you know what his G Point is, onto which you´ll direct your sales presentation.

Once you find the G POINT you never let go of it. When you already know about his hobbies and your clients basic need, then you have to deepen in to it. It´s not the time to sale, it´s the time to deepen. You have to make more questions in order for you to sense the level of detail.

Let´s suppose after you finish talking about their hobby, the person you´re with tells you:

Client: "So, David. Please tell me about your wonderful product."

$uper Seller: "Carolyn, I´d like to ask you some questions before, for me to know what to offer you and to understand what your business needs. Is that ok?"

Client: "Sure, go ahead. What do you need to know?"

So, here is where you begin with the questions to identify needs:

An Analysis Questionnaire to Find A Company´s Need

1. How are things doing in the Company?

2. Do you have general written objectives and goals?

3. Do you have objectives and goals per area?

4. Do you have detailed plans to accomplish objectives?

5. Does the staff participate in the planning?

6. Do you have a general organization chart?
7. Do you have the company´s mission statement and overview written down?

8. Is the staff aware of it?

9. Does it have a written set of job descriptions?

10. Are the duties and responsibilities clearly assigned?

11. Are the job skills required by every position determined?

12. Is the talent selection area focused in hiring personnel who meet the skills required for the position?

13. Is the responsibility to lead and make decisions accepted by the personnel?

14. Does a headquarters and managements performance evaluation system exist?

15. Do the chiefs and managers have the right skills to stablish adequate interpersonal relationships?

16. Is team work working out?

17. Are the policies and procedures stablished in writing?

18. Are there any performance indicators for each of the company´s areas?

19. Does it have a decision-making methodology?

20. Does it have the appropriate communication channels?

"The **secret** for **success** consists in knowing **that which nobody else knows.**" Aristotle

What´s the first appointment´s main objective?

Sum up the need. Based on the questions you made, the thing you will do is repeat to him why you were obviously taking notes of all the reasons they consider necessary to buy from you, like productivity, income improvement, sales improvement, and all the other motives he thinks to be the most important to be able to make a decision. There´s always a G POINT, so, you have to make emphasis in telling him something like:

$uper Seller: "Just to be sure, so, you consider the most important thing in your business is (Mention their G POINT)."

Client: "Yes, that´s correct. The G POINT is the most important thing for me."

Acknowledgment. Thank them for their time. Let that person feel that only for the fact of giving you the chance to be with them, you´re more than satisfied. Let the person know that every minute is valuable and remember to be using his names on numerous occasions in an hour-long appointment, in which you should have at least used his name 50 times."

Thank the person as if they had already bought from you. Let the person feel and know you´re really doing it from the heart."

Schedule the next appointment for the presentation. Once you have thanked them, now is the moment to bring out an appointment, in which based on the G POINT or basic need, you prepare him a presentation. You need to have an exact date. You can´t come out of the office or finish the appointment without having the both of you sat down and checked your work agenda to determine the date for the next appointment in which the next presentation will take place. Ask them if it´s necessary that other people that also make decisions need to be present to evaluate the product or service.

Excited to greet them. Once you schedule the appointment, thank them again, and you can make them a promise, so he knows you´re there to serve and help them.

$uper Seller: "Thanks again "Client", I assure you we´ll help you the (G POINT) is what you´ll be getting from us. Our commitment is helping you fulfill it."

"**Clients** don't expect you to be **perfect**. They expect you to fix things when the get complicated." - Donald Porter

$uper Seller Powers

1. Develop a set of questions for you to determine your client's emotional state and use it in your daily life. Begin practicing with your family and use it with people close to you.
2. Develop a set of questions for you to find the need your product or service can fulfill.
3. Learn how to listen. Try no talking for 15 minutes straight. Meditate so this may help you. Try the Silva Method.
4. Do an exercise with some of your coworkers. Create a round table with 5 or 7 of the best sale people and practice.

5. Do the exercise of randomly scanning your coworkers' offices as if they were your clients, find out their hobbies and ask them about them.
6. Practice sensing the emotions of the people around you.
7. Make a set of questions in order to find what's the basic need or G Point.

POWER = Information + Action

What's the best way to make a presentation?

Presentation based on needs

7

"You must find your **client´s G Point** in order for you to sale them. David Gaona

1. Why you must use the G Point?
2. Why is it important to use data and be versatile in your presentation?
3. What´s the structure for a presentation?

4. What´s a 60 second presentation?

5. What are social styles and VAKS?

6. What do you need to ask after every presentation?

7. $uper $eller Powers

Why you must use the client's G Point in the presentation?

When you prepare the set of questions for the analysis of the client's needs, you have to make sure you find your client's real and basic need, which will cause them to prefer to buy the product or service from you with which you will satisfy them with. That's why it's important for you to take the necessary time to set up the presentation based upon the basic needs. You have to make the presentation last for 1 hour at the most, going very highly, as the human being is only able to maintain continuously focused for 15 minutes only.

The G Point

During the presentation you must mention at least 30 times how you´re going to satisfy the basic need (g point). If it's correct it must be mentioned at least in 30 occasions within an hour. Let's set an example. The client tells you their basic need is to increase their company's productivity. Let's suppose what you´re selling is an administration software, then what you need to do is find at least 10 benefits in which your software fulfills such need. Enlist the benefits and base your presentation on them.

Write down a paper sheet for each benefit and title them with the key word "Productivity," and repeat it constantly within each. Let's say one of the main benefits is that the person in charge of purchases, no longer has to transfer the purchase information from one Excel sheet to the other. So, from taking you 1 hour to do it in Excel, no it takes only 30 minutes. So, you say, "the productivity that will be obtained for purchasing information is about 50%". Also, remember to use the word "productivity" repeatedly. The second benefit would be that the information can be found online, so you speak to them in the following matter: "a productivity increasement from up to 30% due to a 24-hour access from any part of the world." It's very important to constantly mention how you´re going to satisfy their G Point.

It probably seems a little exaggerated to do it so constantly, but I assure you, the client won't notice it, on the contrary, they will feel an affinity with you as you´re speaking their same language. If you think it´s too much, then don´t write it down, but do repeat the word constantly. You have to speak their same language, talk to them about the same needs. Your presentation has to be so versatile it can adjust to any client.

"**People** buy what they **wish** for, not what they **need**."

This one time, I had the chance to visit a client at my coaching company (www.iexito.com) and he had told me he needed help from one of my companies. He told me the basic need was to make more productive and to make it more profitable. At the end of the presentation, he mentioned he didn´t want to start the project yet, even though he needed to. Getting more in to the conversation I realized his most important wish was to go on vacation with his family, as he had 30 years not been able to leave his business and that was where the click was. What he told me from the heart was he wanted to take a vacation. Immediately after we finished talking about where he wanted to go to, that he wanted to go to Europe with his family without having to worry that his business would end because he wouldn´t be there to take care of them. Train yourself with us!

So, that was when he signed up immediately, he told me we would start that same day. as one of our client's promises to them is that they can take a vacation 6 months after we start, and we were able to fulfill him that in our guarantee. He was able to go on vacation. All of this is in order to be able to confirm that people buy what they wish for the more than what they need. That's why it´s important to find that unfulfilled wish or G Point.

Why you should use data?

When you obtain information on the main needs or G point, prepare data from previous and actual clients that will help you sustain as an example that your product or service is the best option.

We'll continue with the same example in which your company sales administration software, you'll have to get information from your actual satisfied clients by asking them for examples in which your software has helped them improve productivity in their companies. You're going to put this information on your presentation without having to name your clients, just tell them something like:

"Client form the Automotive Industry obtained 50% of productivity by improving the response time on quotations."

You need to use examples and it's better to ask your clients if you can use their data, so your potential clients can call them. Remember that your best sales people are your most satisfied customers.

What's a versatile presentation?

Your presentation should last 1 hour at the most (20 minutes presentation, 20 minutes of questions, and 20 minutes for closure). This should be your $uper $eller Standard, and you should also be versatile to adapt if your client wants to see another type of information or demonstration. You have to be prepared for any type of change. As I tell my assisting participants to my courses, my associates, and sales people, you have to be ready to provide everything which the client needs during the presentation, like having a pair of sneakers ready if they want to tour the company. You have to bring a computer if they'd like for you to make a presentation, have your product ready for him to test it, and to have coffee if he needs for you to talk to him.

Take all the stuff you need with you to be able to make a $uper $eller Presentation and to make any adjustments necessary, and please understand that if your client tells you that elephants "fly", even if it's only 2 inches, they "fly". This is the importance of being flexible when presenting. You have to put yourself in your client´s shoes and they have to know your more of an advisor than a sales person. That´s why you need to have a lot of tolerance for frustration and to know that the presentation may take a drastic turn in any moment.

I say to you again, make sure your presentation has the basic need or G Point information and data, and put the company's name everywhere. That the benefits are all impregnated with your client's basic needs and use examples which have already solved that same problem. The most important thing is that you´re conscious that everything can change according to how your client asks. As a $uper $eller, you have to be ready.

What must the Presentation's Structure be like?

Company: Use the first 5 minutes to talk about who you are, talk about the team's experience, your main clients, your most outstanding results. Use examples from other satisfied clients and include the basic G Point need results which you have already resolved with other clients. Do the duty of talking to your satisfied clients and ask them for a favor (with its corresponding commission), that they talk about the success story.

Benefits: Put your product's benefits and impregnate them with the need. Use it at least from 25 to 30 times during your hour of presentation and you have to be ready to change it according to how the sales presentation is resulting.

"Describe your **product** in terms of what it **does**, not in terms **of what it is**." Bryan Tracy

Delivery Times: During the 20-minute presentation, give them delivery times, you need to include them and make questions like: When would you like to have the product in your hands? Or, when would like to begin improving your productivity with our service? In order to have and estimated start-up date, and above all, let them be aware of the delivery times of their services.

Questions: Being a $uper Seller, I respond to most of the questions at the moment they´re asked, except for investments, which I handle at the last part of the presentation. I make sure the client has the information at the moment he requests it, only what refers to investments, I ask the client to wait until I finish. If it's a question about the product, service, or about the benefits, my advice is you answer it the second he makes it.

Investment: The price for the product or service, or better said, the investment, must be given within the last 5 minutes of those 20 that the presentation lasts. It's important to handle the client's pressure and to ask them in the nicest was to allow you to finish the presentation as it is very short, and to show them the benefits after you've finished.

Why should you make your presentation to be practical?

Something that will make your client connect with you immediately, is that you prepare them a practical presentation. If you have a product, give them a live demonstration of what it can do to fulfill their needs. You can show them a video or a presentation with images if its complicated, but it's important it touches the client's G point basic need, that you're presenting them.

Why use testimonials?

The more real testimonies and examples of satisfied clients, the more connection and closure possibility there'll exist. Have a list of satisfied customers you can use as sales people and as examples. 40% of my consulting company come from referrals, which come to me after they visit the clients that have obtained outstanding results thanks to the consulting, we provided them with. In fact, I have my client's results categorized so I can use them, depending on the type of result or need my clients are looking to fulfill. You can also do this by client type or need.

What's the importance of answering questions?

The question session is where the sale really begins. Here is where you need to breathe and really write down the questions you're being asked. For this, you should have already prepared yourself with a list of possible questions they can ask you.

"Satisfy your client's unconscious needs like the need to feel important, valued, and respected. "
Brian Tracy

Being versatile is important and remember to be prepared for any change. That's why it's imperative for you to present your company in 60 seconds, that you're able to give a small review of what you can do with your product or service, so you can schedule a business meeting.

What's a 60 second presentation?

The elevator speech an integral part of your personal brand strategy. It's the trick under your sleeve. In order to be able to sale your products efficiently, it must be so simple and impressive, that the person who's listening decides to take action.

What's an elevator speech?

The speech given shouldn't by an autobiography or a detailed business plan, it´s a small summary of who you are, what you do, and how you can help the person who's listening. It's just you, selling yourself in a simple and concise using a format very familiar to many. Even when your elevator speech is similar to your biography, this must be communicated in a different way, which has a very special and memorable touch.

Who needs one?

People that sale services during the day, such as trainers, advisors, speakers, should have a well-structured speech, well integrated into your marketing plan.

We believe that each person in the business that's dedicated in getting new clients, must know their elevator speech. This is any person that can go to a conference, a networking reunion, a seminar, or any person you bump into an elevator. There's always a good opportunity to generate a good business relationship. The elevator speech prepares you for these opportunities and it equips you with a powerful tool that helps you complete a business meeting.

How to prepare an elevator speech?

Like everything in business, you have to know what's the elevator speech's purpose. It can be to sale consultancy services, to obtain financing for a project, or to get a work interview - you need to focus on who your audience will be. In case you have different professional objectives, you must have different speeches for different situations.

In order to have a good speech, you must make you a several questions, and the answers should be a good start. The questions needed are:

- What's the value it provides?

- How does it provide value?
- What's the differential value of its offer?
- What's its target market?

4 Steps to Create an Excellent Elevator Speech

- Step 1: Start with an action phrase that isn't a noun. ("I am X" - don't use a "tag" - doesn't want people to put it in a box).
- Step 2: Add a sentence about what it does ("I do Y" - How does it help people).
- Step 3: A sentence that IMPACTS. ("People who use my process find Z" - list one or two things that impact your prospect).
- Step 4: It ends with an action ("I'm searching A" - Be clear. If he asks for something not so specific, it's going to be really hard for him to obtain it).

Duration

The best speech should not pass over 60 seconds, which should be around 400 words. Imagine getting up in an elevator on the 0 floor and continue talking till the 8th floor.

Did it catch their attention?

As in any speech, the elevator speech should start with an aim to get the attention from the person listening. This can be a phrase that really makes the person pay attention for 60 seconds. This trick is critical when you're in a networking reunion, and the person you've just met is looking to get connected with another one. Getting attention for 60 seconds is really important.

How clear must you be?

You have to be clear in the speech. It must be understood by any person without them having to be related to the industry, if you use too many technical terms you may get different results.

He will remember

An effort must be done so the speech may be remembered. You can use visual language, or simply be a little different. Its important for the speech to be remembered because it's different. Imagine listening to 30 speeches in an hour, so how can you make possible for your speech to be remembered.

Remember to finish with an action.

At the end of the speech, you must try the other person that listens thinks "How can we do business." One way to do this try and have them contact you, give them your business card or schedule a meeting.

Time to practice

Now that you have a speech ready it's time to practice. Present the speech to your friends, in front of a mirror or in front of a camera. Look forward in failing before presenting to an investor or possible client.

Conclusion

A good elevator speech can be very useful in different situations, like selling your service to a client, getting a job interview, or asking half a million dollars to a person.

"In order to know what people really **think**, pay attention to what they **do**, more than what they **say**." Rene Descartes

Once you´ve finished your 60 second presentation, now we´re going to talk about how to identify the different types of social styles in clients, to know if you have to use a computer and show them the presentation, the safety shoes if you´re going to tour the company, or have coffee ready if you want to talk to him about the results you´ve accomplished with your clients.

What are the social styles you can find in your clients?

People in general have different styles of ways of thinking and doing things. We communicate in different ways with each other, feeling more or less comfortable with some people, and so much with other not knowing why.

Nowadays, we know about 4 social styles: Analytical, Affable, Expressive, and Dynamic. This theory was developed by the psychologists Robert Reid and David Merril in 1963. So, they say, that it's easier and you connect better with people of your same social style: affable with affable or expressive with expressive, and so on.

In this process, people from each style approach their jobs and lives in general in different ways.

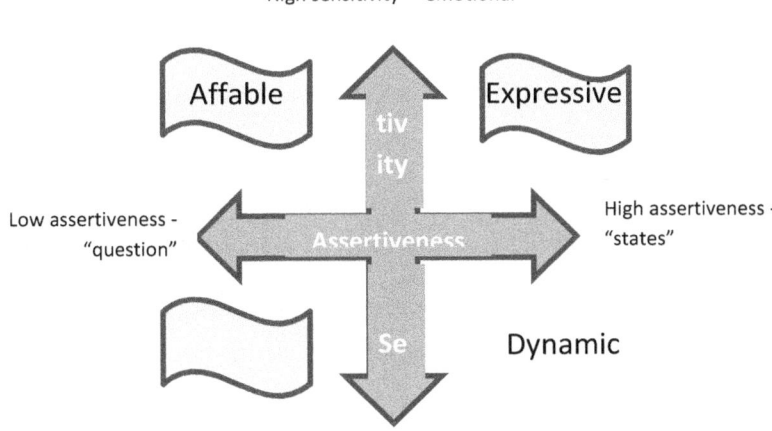

Analytical

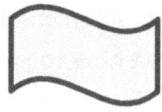

What's versatility? It's the way others notice a person is willing to abandon its own behavior within their "comfort zone", with the sole purpose of collaborating more efficiently with others. It's the way you work well with others, regardless of their own personal style.

Versatility is not a set of behaviors set aside from its style. People are versatile through the prism of their style.

There are two key steps to understand the relation between style and versatility: First of all, it's necessary for each person to understand their own style and other's that work with you, what I mean is, "know yourself" and "know others." Keeping this in mind, we can say you will understand other people's needs as well as your own.

In this point, you can adjust your behaviors in order to work more efficiently with others getting unsuspected results.

When others see a great deal of versatility in you, they notice you come out of your comfort zone by modifying behaviors in order to work harmoniously with the team you're working with.

Once you've done these exercises, the people who you work with will give you a certain type of feedback. It may not be right away, as sometimes it takes time for people's perceptions to join to a change of behavior. At least, at first, maybe they won't even talk about it, but they'll give you feedback about your behavior one way or the other, and this is and indicator of your versatility.

Some of the questions that can help you understand and get to know better the level of versatility in which you're currently are:

Do the people that work with you enjoy doing so? Do they feel comfortable talking and exchanging information? If the answers are yes, then you have a high level of versatility, if not, then you have to get out of your comfort zone, by modifying your behaviors so others can see you close to them and working more effectively with others as well.

By getting to know your clients better, you'll have a great advantage over your competition, as it gets you a step further in order to capitalize sales management.

In order to get to know you clients, there are several tools that work really well, for example, Pit Nelson colors four general types of consumer personalities which are represented in a matrix that helps you offer your products in a more assertive way in a dynamic market, such as massive consumption outlets.

On his side, William Mourton Martson, develops in 1928, in his publishing of Emotions of Normal People, a personalities assessment tool - well known as profile - called DISC, which us currently being mainly used in Human Resources. Although, when applied in the commercial area, it becomes a powerful tool which allows you to understand your clients better and to get the proper products close to them. In 1964, Doctor David W. Roger Merril and Roger Reid started an investigation that focused on developing a model that could anticipate the sales success and career management, which was developed and presented by Doctor James W. Taylor as a "Social Style Matrix."

With this matrix, according to the assertiveness and sensitivity of the different types of personalities, you can get four different kinds of clients with the following characteristics.

Expressive Client:

1. Wear fashion and brand clothing.
2. Prefer flashy colors.
3. Look for innovative products.
4. Can be kind of a kidder and sarcastic.
5. Can be charismatic but arrogant.
6. Not very worried about the price.

Affable Client:

1. Dress up comfortably with bright colors.
2. Are very kind and courteous.
3. Talks about their family.
4. **Look for guarantees.**

Dynamic Client:

1. Dress conservatively and prefer dark colors.

2. Know well that they want-
3. Are very direct but not so kind.
4. Are interests in prices.

Analytical Client:

1. Regularly dress conservatively.
2. Ask a lot of questions.
3. Analyze the product's services.
4. **Prefers to be shown through facts and in writing.**

By making a consumer analysis and grouping them according to each of the group's features found in the Social Styles Matrix. It's much easier to direct the efforts and sales to the main decision makers. For example:

How to sale to an expressive client?

1. Get their attention using a main idea (use audiovisual presentations).
2. Show them how the product can get personal status and personal achievement.
3. Show them the product in a creative way.
4. Show him the product is innovative and they are the first ones to used it.
5. Use direct closures and by choice.
6. Be interested in what the client's saying.

7. It's easy to do Cross-Selling and Up-Selling (in case of having a very diverse product and services portfolio).

How to sale to an affable client?

1. Be relaxed and kind.
2. Offer guarantees.
3. Show them the products based on the improvements the client and their families can obtain.
4. Be concrete during the presentation.
5. Use direct closures.
6. Don't lose control over the sale (it's very easy to lose control and deviate the objective by talking about way to personal things).
7. Push the closure.
8. It´s easy to do an Up-Selling.

How to sale to a dynamic client?

1. Show them the product in a concrete way.
2. Look for sensing the needs in a really quick and precise way.
3. Make emphasis in your product or service's cost-benefit.
4. Use closure by choice.
5. Don't try to impose your point of view.
6. Don´t push the closure.
7. It's easy to do an Up-Selling.

How to sale to an analytical client?

1. Use facts, principals and logic.
2. Use and take notes of the product's unique aspects.
3. Show the products benefits with written support.
4. Make emphasis on long term benefits.
5. Use direct closures.
6. Be good in identifying what the question is and don´t give away too much information.
7. It's easy to do Cross-Selling and Up-Selling.

It's important to understand that users in each segment don't exist, for which it's suggested to carry on with key accounts segmentation.

The main message is: to know your clients well, know your market well, know your product well, because selling is making your client to buy in an intelligent way.

Now that you know which are the social styles and understand you have to make differences in the presentation. Another important aspect is to know we communicate in three different ways: some people are visual, auditive, kinesthetic, and sensory.

What are the different types of communication you can find in your clients?

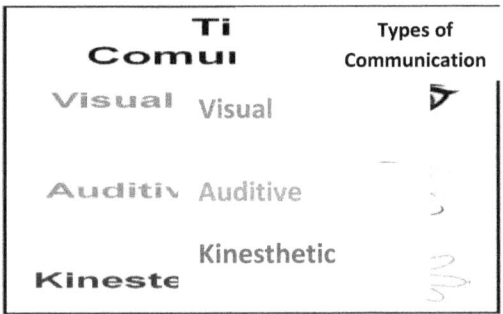

Visual

How they talk?

Visual people talk a lot using their hands, their body, and they move a lot. They use expressions like did you see that?, watch this, or are you seeing this? They're people that express a lot through their eyes, they pay lots of attention if you talk to them up front and you're watching them.

How they learn?

Visuals like to learn a lot by looking and watching movies or computers, and they like to check out landscapes.

How does their environment look like?

Their environment is very organized, everything checks out, like colors and shapes. It's really a very visually harmonious environment.

How they dress?

They dressed very combined from the shoes, sucks, underwear, necklace. All the colors are flashy, and the brands are very important.

What are their hobbies?

1. Painting.
2. Drawing.
3. Movie Theater.
4. Walk in the park.
5. Watch movies.
6. Watch TV.
7. Watch the Sunset.

How to sale to them?

1. You have to make them a presentation.
2. They have to see.
3. It it's possible, take them to the battlefield to check out the product or service in action.
4. Show them graphics.

5. Make emphasis in the visual environment.

Auditive

How they talk?

They use words like listen, do you hear? are you listening? or I heard you. They either talk too slow or too loudly, they use very sophisticated words and remember everything you told them, and they usually listen or talk to you sideways in order to pay attention.

How they learn?

They enjoy listening to audio books, conferences, attending courses, they want you to speak to them.

How is their environment?

It's not so visually organized, but they usually have soft music or quietness. They like to feel comfortable in their environment no matter how it looks like.

How they dress?

They dress well but not as good visuals. They're the ones that pay less attention to clothing.

What are their hobbies?

1. Listening to music.
2. Talking.
3. That you speak to them.
4. Listening to nature.
5. Listening to radio.
6. Playing an instrument.
7. Dancing.

How to sale to them?

1. You have to talk to them.
2. Play them a video with an auditive experience.
3. Give them data.
4. Pay attention to what you´re saying.
5. Use tones of voice accordingly to how the speak.
6. Use spoken client testimonials or videos.
7. Play them music or use silence.

Kinesthetic

How they talk?

They talk recklessly and very fast, they like things immediately, they´re always in a hurry and can run over people or even curse. They tend to greet you and either give you a massage or a strong slap on the back.

How they learn?

They learn by doing, they have to do it in order to learn it.

How is their environment?

Their environment is very comfortable, it doesn´t matter if their space is disorganized as long as it´s comfortable. The chair may be broken, but if it feels good that´s what matters.

How they dress?

They dress very comfortably, use comfortable shoes, brands don´t matter, only comfort. They can use the same pants and shirt as long as they're comfortable.

What are their hobbies?

1. Do exercise.
2. Walking.
3. Visiting natural areas.
4. Hugging.
5. Giving massages.
6. Receiving massages.

How to sell to them?

1. Let them check the product.

2. Do and undo whatever they want with it, so they get excited by using the product or service with their own hands.
3. Take them to the field to check the product.
4. An interactive video.

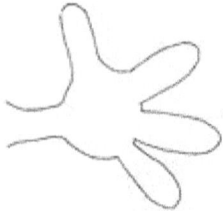

Sensory

How they talk?

Sensorial people will talk to you a lot about scents, how good it smells, what a nice music. What they do is to pay to much attention to the sensations placed in the surroundings.

How they learn?

They learn through scents, with sensations, with light, with music, you need to activate them all their senses.

How is their environment?

Their environment is just very harmonious, and they pay lots of attention to scents.

How they dress?

They smell good and dress well.

What are their hobbies?

1. They have a combination of all.

How to sale to them?

1. They have a combination of all.

It's very important you get the ability to detect your client in order to sale him adequately. For me, there's no kind of people who doesn't make any chemistry, and what's simple happening is that you're not communicating with them adequately, if it's either your couple, son, father, client, etc. You have to learn how to communicate adequately. Practice is key, first analyze the people around you. Make a plan of how to make chemistry as a common denominator of activities, it's like love. Do some activities in group, and then, satisfy the need with the adequate communication, and so it happens.

It's the same in any relationship, whether is sales or emotional. You have to learn to communicate and be an excellent actor depending on the situation found and the person you have in front of you.

Why to tell jokes and stories?

Man learns better with stories than with speeches. As a $uper Seller you have to learn to tell stories, put some drama into them, that if the client wants to know more about some products, you learn data and stories about your clients, so you can tell them with a high level of detail. Learn to tell them like you tell stories to your children. With the right tones of voice, the right words that will make your client's skin crawl.

Jokes are also an important part within your presentation. Just make sure your client likes jokes. 1 out of 100 businesspeople like jokes and have a good sense of humor. It´s important to kid around for when your client and the environment requires it.

"Spend lots of time talking to your clients face to face. You'll be surprised to know how many companies don´t listen to their clients." Ross Perot

Once you're able to identify the type of communication your client uses, now you have to learn how to read your client's non-verbal communication, for you to know where to get him when you´re closing a sale.

Did you know 80% of communication is non-verbal?

80% of communication is non-verbal. 10% is the tone, 10% are the words you say, which means, a person tells you more with what he does and how he acts, than with what he says. With this, you have to analyze, as a $uper Seller, each step you client takes during the presentation and closure. You have to know his gestures and each word you say will have an impact on his person.

There are 4 parts within non-verbal communication:

1. The first part is determined by their arms and legs.

If their arms or legs are closed or open. If you're making a presentation and your client has their arms or legs closed, this means he's closed, and he doesn't want to receive information. It doesn't mean he's cold, or comfortable, or any of those things. Remember 98% of our thoughts are governed by our subconscious brain, so if there's something we don't like, our brain gives us an immediate response of pain and protects our most vulnerable parts like the heart and genitals. You must learn that the more open your client has their hands and arms, the more receptive and open they will receive information of our product and service. If they cross their hands, then give them a pen and ask them to write something down so they uncross them.

When **people talk, listen** to them completely- Ernest Hemmingway

2. The second part is visual contact.

Either way you look, your client also determines in great measure if they're telling the truth or not. Make sure to observe your client's sight when your making key questions. In the part from above, it explains where the eyes look to when a person is answering a question and what does it mean.

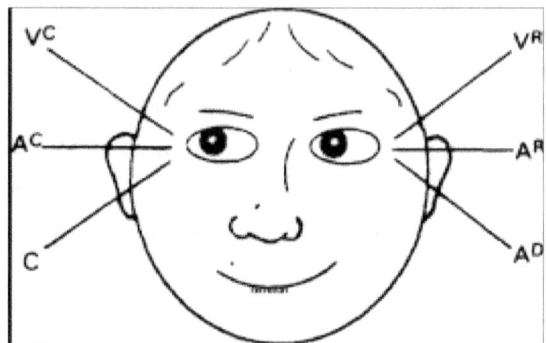

Neurological studies have demonstrated the eye movement is associated with the activation of different parts of the brain. The eye is connected to the brain through a nerve, and this can access different areas of the brain without have the need to.

They discovered that, in order to search for images remembered, most people move their eyes upstream to the left. In order to create new images, something they haven't lived through, they move their eyes to the right, as it's the channel for dreams, projects, and creativity.

When somebody seeks for a sound they remember, they'll move their eyes to the left at the height of the ear, and when they try to create a new sound or imaging it, their eyes will move to the right. This is the channel for composers, musicians, presenters while creating their presentation, etc.

If the person needs to solve a problem, ask themselves about a certain situation and make conclusion, they will lower their eyes to the left, and if they want to get in touch with their feelings, they'll lower their sight to the right. If their feelings are of depression, anguish, fear, sadness, it's better to leave that channel by moving the eyes to a different side.

Being conscious of eye movements can help us move our eyes to where we need to. Examples:

- When we need to remember something, by moving our eyes upstream to the left, will provide us with the information we need more rapidly. This applies better with people who have bad memory.

- When we need to do projects, by moving our eyes upstream to the right, it'll be much easier to do so imagining the results.

- When we have a problem and we need to solve it or generate options, the right thing to do is move our eyes downstream to the left, and there we'll find the answers we seek, where the analysis channel is.

- When we found ourselves in an unfavorable mood, by being conscious our eyes mustn't go down to the right, will increase the sensation.

The conscious eye movement is a way of discovering how our brain works. Even, through our eye keys, with practice, we can teach our brain new ways in order to correct undesirable behaviors, attitudes, or reactions. By "looking" at the right side when seeking information, it can be a very useful skill.

3. The third part are sitting, gestures, and postures.

Always sit in front of the person, just ask first the place you'll be sitting in, but after this, look forward to sitting down in front of your client. Also, read the client's postures, as the sales posture is always an interesting one. How does an interested person sit? He sits with a forward lean.

By showing interest or by touching their face as if analyzing information, reading which part of the face they touch, has everything to do with a sale. If they touch their chin and lean forward, they have all their interest in what you're showing them. But if you see them touching their eyes and robbing them, it means they don't want to see, so go ahead and ask them some questions, like, may I continue? Or, do you have any questions I can answer? If he touches his nose it means he doesn't like how it smells. It might be your presentation, or the price, or something, but it's your task to ask him some questions.

If they touch their mouth it means they want to say something, so it's important you let them speak. If they touch their ears it means they don't want to listen, so there's something you said they didn't like. No precisely because you spoke inappropriately, but because it's possible due to the situation they're going through.

4. The fourth part is the tone of voice and the word emphasis.

If the client talks to you in low tones about certain things, there are some of them they yell out. Then, you have to pay attention to this words or sentences, behind these there's lots of information you can use in order to sale or help them. Copy their tone of voice and use the same words.

80% of communication is non-verbal, 10% of it is the tone, and 10% are the words you use. So, you better shut up and let the client do the talking. So, learn how to master your non-verbal communication and your body language.

"Develop the **habit of listening** and let the **client rule** the conversation." Brian Tracy

You must always, but always, at the end of a presentation, while you're in your car, do the learning questionnaire. Whether you sold or not, you must always answer the following learning questionnaire.

Why is it important to prepare a presentation for men and another for women?

You have to learn, as a $uper Seller, that women talk 3 times more than men do. Women like details, they like for you to tell them things with stories and that you take all the time in the world. It's completely different to sale to a man or a woman, so, prepare two different presentations, one long and one short.

It's not a secret that women talk more than men do, which was basically verified by American neuropsychiatrist Louann Brizendine, who concluded women speak 13 thousand more words daily than men do, which is also provoked by a protein present in the body called FOXP2, better known as "the language protein."

Mega Health's psychologist, Ricardo Bascuñán, pointed out in It Could Be Something Else, there are lots of elements in this research which are easily explainable. Besides analyzing genes, we have to check where the woman comes from and their environment, and that they talk more doesn't mean what they say has less content or is less relevant.

"Women effectively talk more because they tend to focus on details that men regularly don´t see. By being immersed in a world which demands them to look good, being a good house wife, where you have to adapt and do it correctly, they experience other aspects of reality. Logically, they see more details that masculinity will ever do." Pointed out the professional.

"On the other hand, the world has taken care of making life easier to men," Bascuñán said, who also mentioned "the right thing is what kind of studies make notice that different biologies will process experiences differently."

This also explains why women don´t agree with a concise answer and why they assure that men "don´t know how to lie." "Women have much more communication skills than men do." The professional finally said.

What you need to ask after each presentation?

Remember that the quality of the questions you make will determine the quality of success you'll obtain. Questions will give a solution for each problem and a lesson for each defeat.

"I always win or learn, I never lose." David Gaona

The first thing you need to ask yourself is What happened? You made a sale or didn´t. If you sold, what happened during the sale? Was it easy or difficult? If you didn´t sale anything then, what happened during the sale? What can you rescue from the meeting or sales presentation you just did.

The second question you need to ask yourself is **What went well?** There's always something which, if it worked, you need to learn whether you made a sale or not, you ask yourself, what did work? In order to keep doing it and celebrating what, if you've done well, and there's lots of things you've done well by the simple fact of attending the sales presentation, which means you did something right.

The third question is **What didn't go well?** You need to identify what you didn't do right during the sale in order to improve it. Make a list of what you'd do better if you could turn back time. You must work in the areas of opportunity and it's better to correct them when you finish the presentation. Make a list and a work plan, and make sure next time you present, you do it better. But there'll always exist an improvement area.

The last question is What did I learn? You need to learn something immediately after you finish, whether you made the sale or not, we can always learn. It's possible if you sold something, you could have sold more, or that presentation was too long. Or that you talked too much, or that if you didn't sale anything, what did you learn, as you always learn something.

<u>The Interrogation</u>

What happened?

What went well?

What didn't work?

What did I learn?

SALES CHECKLIST

1. Clothing according to the customer.
2. Tooth brush, tooth paste, cologne, and deodorant.
3. Spare Clothing.
4. Computer.
5. Hard drive and USB.
6. Projector.
7. Notebook and pen to take notes.
8. Tissues.
9. Phone book.
10. Presentation according to social communication and style.
11. Security shoes.
12. Tennis shoes and comfortable clothing.
13. Short presentation.
14. Testimonial list.
15. Data from the company you're working for.
16. Magnifying glass and camera.
17. Learning notebook.
18. Sales Books.
19. Sales Audio books.
20. Color pens to take notes.
21. Wireless internet.
22. Stationery and contacts.

$uper Seller Powers

1. Make your 60 second presentation and present your product 10 times to your salespeople's round table. Practice it all the time with all the people you find.
2. Develop you telephone script and test it 3 times. Carry out statistics.
3. What do you need to ask yourself after each closure?
    a) What happened?
    b) What went well?
    c) What didn't work?
    d) What did I learn?
4. Make a list of possible questions your client can make and how to solve them.
5. Have a list of example testimonies or clients so they can help you in the sales process.
6. Make a list of data the client may ask of your product or service.

7. **Have a different presentation for each social style, communication type, or different ones for men or women.**

What's the most powerful closure?

Aprendiendo
a cerrar

8

"The best way to **close a sale** is to **shut up**, make some **questions**, and to sale when the **client tells you to**." David Gaona

1. What's the closure efficiency?
2. Why is he not a yes?
3. What's shut up and sale?
4. What are yes-type questions?
5. How do you handle any objection?
6. What are your businesses' objections?
7. $uper Seller Powers

What's a closure?

A sales closure is the peak moment within the process when all efforts must be compensated, but in this one is when most sales people fail. Why? But the simplest reason that they don't know how to close, they don't memorize the closure, besides the lack of practice and fear of being rejected.

Closure is a probability, just pure math. If you want to increase your sales, you need to play with your closure numbers. For example, you need to keep a record of how many people you present to, every day you make presentations. This will help you see your results more objectively, so you realize it's only a matter of time for you to sale.

"When the **questions** begin is when the **sale** really begins. A question is like a trigger for the **client** to **buy**." David Gaona

What do I mean by this? Let's suppose you made 20 presentations and 2 sales during the week, which is a closure effectivity of 10%, and this Is the number by which all your sales actions should be ruled, and all phone calls, presentations, referrals, and collections should come from.

If you made 20 presentations and closed 2, and you want to have 10 closures, you need to make 100 presentations per week. If you made 5 phone calls for each presentation, then you need to make 500 phone calls. It's a simple numeric game.

What's Sales Closure Efficiency?

The important thing here is being effective in sales closure "**SCE**", as this will determine the earnings you receive through sales. So, make sure you know how many calls you make. What's your phone call efficiency? I mean, how many gave you an appointment for you to give them a presentation, and from those presentations, how many did you close or sold to? Thanks to this, you'll be calm regarding decision making, for its easy to know that in order to sale 1 product or service you need to make 5 presentations, so your focus will change completely. Besides, it gets to be much more fun when you do it knowing you'll obtain a result and that your results depend on how fast you move.

Sales Closure Efficiency			
Calls	Presentations	Sales	SCE
100	10	2	20%

"In order to be **successful in sales**, you simply need to talk to lots of people every day. And the exciting thing about it is, that there's **lots of people** to talk to!" Jim Rohn

What does the word NO mean?

The word **NO**. You have to understand as a sales person it means something much more different than what most people mean. These two letters really mean yes, but on another time, they mean yes, but you have to try and do it in a better way. They mean yes, but you have to present to me 10 more times. They're not an improvement opportunity, it means they won't buy from you in this moment, but probably later they will. It means yes, but you didn't use the right words. It means I need time to think about it. It really means **YES.**

"The **sales** department should take lessons from their kids. What does the word "**no**" to a **kid**? Almost nothing." Jim Rohn

Closure is answering questions to your client, It's the questions a person has about your product or service. It means during the presentation you didn't read your client correctly enough so the closure would include so many questions, but that's just a part of sales, the client will always have questions before he buys from you. Only sometimes there are more questions than others, it really depends on how well you do the previous steps. The better the contacts you get and that they're referrals, the higher probability the closure will take place and the amount of questions will be less. It also depends on how well you detect your client's point G opportunities, and how well you satisfy them in the sales presentation, how well you use testimonies and presenting with data, will determine how easy you'll close a sale. If you do well during the first steps, it'll help you lower the timing and amount of questions and doubts your client may have.

Closure consists on your clients' questions and doubts, and that you have to train to resolve, you have to transfer that emotion and help him make a decision. If you train like a $uper Seller, you'll have these closures' information in order to help your client, and this is a skill you obtain first by memorizing the closures, and second, by practicing them now. Practice will help you use these tools as if you were a natural born sales person. Memorize these closures and start using them now, you need to use them on time in the right circumstances, but you have to have them in your hand the whole time, so you can use them. I set them up for you in an acronym, so you can remember them easily, "CLOSING."

"Once I've conquered a victory, I never use the same strategy for the second time, but, under the circumstances, I vary my methods to infinity."
Sun Tzu

Close your mouth and sell.

Link the buyer or client to what you're selling.

Option elimination until they find the right one.

Swing the question right back to them.

Invincible Rhino use them as advisors to tell you what they want.

Not the right answer, give them a wrong date so they correct you and say yes.

Go on selling, the best time to sale is when you just did it.

What are the 7 most powerful closures that exist?

Close your mouth and Sell.

Which is it?

Like the name says, it's the most powerful of all. When a client wants to buy, you don't make him a presentation, you don't show him the product, you don't talk to him, you don't explain him the benefits. The only thing you do is sell him. You need to use the closure very well and for it to be the one you use better. There's lots of clients that don't want to sell even when the client wants to buy them. Please! If the client wants to buy form you, just Close your mouth and sell!

When do you use it?

This is used when the client has already decided, and doesn't want an explanation, he just wants you to give him the product or service. He's desperate, and regularly gets to the store or office yelling for you to sell him. You only need to offer him more than 2 or 3 products, but first sell him.

"The only **pressure** felt during a **professional sales presentation** must be the silence that occurs after you make a **closing question**." Brian Tracy

Link the buyer or client to what you're selling.

Which is it?

In the linking closure, suggest you client to imagine themselves using your product or service, mention them things like: "when your product arrives," or "when you're driving the car," you need to get the client involved by having them imagine themselves using the product or service. It's also important you do it using your product or service, let them feel it and have the experience of using it. This takes lots of imagination and if it's possible to have them use the product and feel it in their hands it would be much better.

When do you use it?

You need to use this all the time, you need your client to desire it, to imagine it several times, and if possible that they use it as well. Let him open the package if it's packed and remember to use all of this all the time.

Option elimination until they find the right one.

Which is it?

This closure is when you give clients two or three options for them to choose, and logically, you have to learn to make them the right questions. For example, if you're selling them a car, what you ask them is "would you like a luxury or a mid-level car?" Always remember to include the most expensive product you have and manage them options where you direct them to where you want them to. Or, for example, would you like your product to arrive on August 10 or 11? Give them several options so they feel they're making the decision.

When do you use it?

When the client wants to buy, but doesn't decide to act, or has some questions about the delivery date, you need to be very intelligent and have the options in your hands, so you help them make a decision.

Swing the question right back to them.

Which is it?

This is the closure when the clients give you a strong objection like: "they told the car had mechanical malfunctions." Then you answer them back with a swing back question like if I show you the car has the least mechanical malfunctions in the market, would you take it? Or If I extend to you the guarantee 1 more year, would you buy it?

When do you use it?

You use it when the clients are bombing you with objections and you have answer them one after the other, so you take that energy and swing it right back to them.

"It is pure **foolishness** to do one thing in the **same way** and expect a different **result**."
Robert Milliken

Invincible Rhino use them as advisors to tell you what they want.

Which is it?

This is something that is most used in the network marketing industry. It's when it's taking you 1 hour to close a client, and suddenly you say to them you're leaving, you start to pack your things and ask them if they can give you feedback as it's clear they're very experienced people? So, they'll start explaining and tell you to use more data and graphs. So, you ask them, did I forget to include more data then? To what they'll answer positively to, and that's where you can use another closure for the objection you need was left behind.

When do you use it?

This is used when one of the closures didn't work, and it's one of the master closures, as you use the client to tell you how to close the sale.

Not the right answer, give them a wrong date so they correct you and say yes.

Which is it?

The not the right answer closure is when you give clients the wrong dates or information on purpose or offer them a more expensive model or service than the one they were interested in. It works like this, you're going to tell them, "so, mister client, you would like us to start the consulting project on the first week of January, right? To what they will answer, "no, I would like to have it the third week of January." So, that is when you just closed the sale.

When is it used?

When the client already decided and gave you a purchase date, but they're just thinking too much about it.

Go on selling, the best time to sale is when you just did it.

Which is it?

This is something most people won't use, and it happens once you already made a sale. This is the best moment to continue offering your product or service, and here is when your energy is at its highest peak. This is when your clients are going to feel like you're a $uper Seller, and that is when you must continue selling. First celebrate, but later, look forward in selling more products to your client, and if not, ask him for referrals and continue selling. At least make some phone calls.

When is it used?

Every time you made a sale, you need to use that energy to sale more. Remember, it's those moments when you feel better and have more energy.

What's an extra closure?

It's the closure of filling out the stationery for the sale.

Which is it?

It's very simple but powerful, just take the contract or the stationery already filled out, for when the moment of closure arrives you pull it out and complete it along with the client. Try to fill out as much as possible and don´t stop until you make the closure.

When is it used?

It's used when the client is undecided and has told you he needs to think about it. It's the moment to bring out the stationery and fill out till you close.

What are yes-type questions?

You have to make yes-type questions during the closure. You need to make sure your client at least tells you yes 30 times during the 60-minute presentation. Yes-type questions are obvious, so the client warms up and says yes at the moment of the purchase of closure. Once you start doing them how this makes the closure much easier, as you have been preparing it during the presentation. They must be questions in which you know the answer must be yes.

1. It's hot isn't it?
2. Traffic is really heavy uh?
3. Is your company of plastics?
4. Your company sales more plastic products, right?
5. You're from Monterrey, right?
6. You're married, right?
7. You like playing basketball, right?
8. You went to college to Tec de Monterrey, right?

Yes-type questions will be working you client out, so you can close the sale. The more yes-type questions, the more probability of closure.

When you find an objection please follow these 10 steps in order to handle objection. These steps are always useful, and you can use them every time somebody says no or asks you a question about your product or service.

What are the 10 steps to handle any objection like a $uper Seller?

1. Ignore the objection and don't take it personal: Remember the clients have their fears, so ignore what they said that made you feel bad or if they said no.

2. Listen carefully: Always listen carefully to what they just said to you, listen to them at least for 1 minute straight until they tell you everything about it.

3. Comment about the last thing they said: Comment about what they just said and repeat to them what they just said so you show them you're paying attention: For example, "Mr. Client, so you think my product or service is too expensive, right?"

4. Ask about the objection: Once you repeat what they just said, then you ask them "why do you think that our service is expensive?" "Compared to whom?"

5. Answer the objection: Once you have enough information, now you give them enough info regarding the objection. For example, "Mr. Client, I agree with you it's expensive compared to our competition. but I want you to understand that if you

want to pay for it in three months, we'll have a return of investment twice faster than the other suppliers you're comparing us with. And look, here I have some information to back up my commentary." (Here is when you use testimonies).

6. Align the objection: Here is when you make sure the client doesn't have any more questions, and you align so all their questions are answered.

7. Change the objection for a question: If they ever give you an objection, then you start asking them questions about the abjection they told you about.

8. Answer the objection: it's the same as in step 5.

9. Closure: Here is when you use all the CLOSURES, until one of them works.

10. Assume the sale is possible at all times, remember No=Yes.

What are the main objections found in your business or service?

All objections are the same, disregarding the product or service, end up in the same spot, money, trust in the product or service, there's no apparent need, they need to check it with somebody else. The main task here is you learn to answer them and give options to your clients and direct them as $uper Sellers to give them options in how to sale help them. Here the key is preparation, ask yourself this question, what would be an objection in my business and what tools can I use to answer them?

> **"Every sale has 5 main obstacles, there's no need, no money, no desire, no trust."** Zig Ziglar

1. Has no money: So, prepare to give them options, like, credit card payment, financing options, let them give you advances, and preparing is key, so, give them 3 options where it's impossible for them to say no.

> **"Price is always a problem, only if you sound just like the rest of the world."** Paul Di Modica

2. Check it with another person: Most "regular" sellers buy this one, but $uper Sellers don't. We know the clients won't check anything out, they're simply telling you how convincing you were. If they really need to check it with somebody else, just go with him where you need to go and present there in that moment if possible.

3. You have to try the product out: Preparing is key, you have to take your product package, prepare videos with more detail about the use of your product or service. use testimonies. For each thing he asks you for, you need a tool you can use.

4. Doesn't need it at the time: It's important the lack of desire never appears here. You always have to think in how to make the client want more, like productivity, health, wealth, etc. Whatever humans may need, they'll want more, so, work in how to answer this objection and create the need.

5. There's no trust: Present the testimonies of popular people, let them sale for you, but as in all cases, preparing is key. Prepare you tool briefcase as a $uper Seller and use it at the right moment.

What do you need to ask yourself after every closure?

The first question you need to ask is what happened? Did you make a sale or not? If you did, what step during the sale was easy or complicated? If you didn't, what happened during the sale? What can you rescue from the meeting or the sales presentation you just read?

The second question you have to ask is **what went well?** There's always something that, if it did work, you must learn whether you made a sale or not. So, ask yourself, what did work? in order to keep doing it and celebrate what you have done right, because, without a doubt, there's many things you've done really well. By the simple fact of going to the sales presentation means you've done something right.

The third question is **what didn't work?** You have to identify what didn't go well during the interview in order to improve it. Make a list of what you can improve if you turn back time, work on the areas of opportunity and the best thing is to correct them when you finish your presentation. Make a list and working plan and make sure next time you present you do it better, but there'll always be an area of opportunity.

The last question is **what did I learn?** As soon as you learned something, whether you made a sale or not. We always learn and it´s possible, if you made a sale, you learned you could've learned more sold even more. Maybe it took you too long presenting, or you talked too much, or if you didn't sale. Also, what did you learn? You can always learn something.

$uper Seller Powers

1. Memorize the sales closures:
   1. **C**lose your mouth and sell.
   2. **L**ink the buyer or client to what you're selling.
   3. **O**ption elimination until they find the right one.
   4. **S**wing the question right back to them.
   5. **I**nvincible Rhino use them as advisors to tell you what they want.
   6. **N**ot the right answer, give them a wrong date so they correct you and say yes.
   7. **G**o on selling, the best time to sale is when you just did it.

2. Answer the 10 main objections to your business.

3. Prepare testimonies and client examples that have already gotten the results.

4. Practice the closures daily with a group of sales people.

5. Make some cards that include the closures and learn them.

6. Listen to the audio about closures from Universidad de la Calle.

7. Ask somebody to give you feedback on your closing skills and presentations.

Did you know our results' guarantee will give up to 30% more on your sales?

Request
payment and
results'
guarantee

9

"**Sales** are a **process, collecting** is a part of it so learn to **enjoy it.**" Phillip Kottler

1. What are the steps you need to be aware of in order to request payment?
2. Why are there companies that sale so much but go bankrupt?
3. What's client service?
4. Why does it help you gain your client's trust?
5. What's a results' guarantee?
6. Why should you always give a guarantee?
7. $uper Seller Powers

I've had the opportunity to work in my consulting company along with clients from China, The United States, Mexico, Argentina, Panama, Peru, Dominican Republic, etc.

There's something which most companies hurt from and this is the process of collecting payments from their clients. In 30% of the companies, collections, which are the pending charges for the product's or service's sales, are very high. A number to be alarmed of within a company would be 30% of past due portfolio. This would mean that if you sold 10 million dollars, 3 million were left pending. This number strongly impacts the sales process and in general the whole operation within the company.

Something we really emphasis about in our company is when we're giving the business training is that selling never stops until we get the client's payment. It's not only when they receive the product, or when they say yes, or we ship the product. The business process should include until the money enters the bank.

That's when a real sale is made. For this, the importance as a business person or a sales person, make sure part of the procedure is collecting the money. Write down a procedure where you stipulate all payments between the client and you.

What are the aspects to look after in the payment process?

The guidelines to follow up in general are the following:

1. Method of payment, credit card, or cash.
2. Payment account.
3. Payment time.
4. Receipt of product against payment.
5. Delivery time.
6. Financing, if you have it.
7. Product guarantee.
8. Non-payment penalties.

Why is it important to request payment? Simply because without your clients' payments on time, the whole company's financial statement will be affected, and all these financial aspects will shake you if you don't have a good collections procedure in your company:

1. In the profit margin.
2. Salary payments.
3. Sales people's payments.
4. Interest on loans.

It's really important you pay attention to the collections subject in your business. Remember sales end until the money enters the bank.

Get your sales people used to expect their commissions until the collecting is done. I know many companies pay their sales people's commissions for being afraid of losing the sale or the sales person. They'd rather get into debt and lower the profit margin. This type of financing is unsustainable, you must pay the sales person until the sale is done. If you're a salesperson make sure your client pays, so give them follow up as well as an excellent service.

Why are there so many companies that sale so much but end up bankrupt?

1. Their expenses are too high.
2. Their accounts receivable is of 15%.
3. They sale products with marginal earnings.
4. They have too much inventory and their cash flow are low.

I want you to compare that to sale a lot doesn't necessary mean that you're a successful business.

Why do you need to systematize the collections process?

Because this will make the company's cash flow increase, so you have to work on your sales department, so it has the systematized collections and you don't have to be worried about it anymore. Make sure your clients are adequate, even if you sale them a lot. But if their payment timing is 3 months, then you have to understand they're financing from you, so look for clients that pay, even if you give them a discount, but in a short time. Although there's occasions in which you have no choice, so look that your collections system is as efficient as possible.

What's client service and why is it important?

The more the competition increases, the products offered in the market will be more diverse and the consumers will be more exigent. They no longer only seek good prices or quality, they seek good client service.

Client service is the service or attention a company or business offer their clients at the moment of answering queries, orders, or claims, sale them a product or deliver it to them.

In order to understand the concept better, we'll see the elements that intervene in client service:

Kindness: it's referent to a kind, courteous, and helpful treatment, and it occurs, for example, when the employees greet the client with a sincere smile, let them know they're there to help, and make them feel that they're genially interested in satisfying their needs before selling them.

Personal Attention: It's the direct and personal attention that considers the client's particular needs, tastes, and preferences, and it occurs, for example, when an employee takes care of them during the whole sales process, when the clients receive a product specially designed to fit their needs, tastes, and particular preferences.

Speed of Attention: It's the speed in which the client's orders are taken, their product is delivered, or their queries or claims are taken care of. This happens, for example, when the company has simple but efficient processes, when it has a sufficient number of employees, and when the person al is qualified to give a rapid attention.

Friendly environment: It's a comfortable environment in which the client feels satisfied, and it occurs, for example, when the employees give them a kind and friendly treatment, when the business premises has a suitable decoration, illumination, and nice music.

Comfort: It refers to the comfort the clients receive when the visit the premises, and it occurs, for example, when the premises have a large enough space, so the clients feel at ease, having comfortable chairs and armchairs, large tables, parking lot, and a place where they can keep their belongings.

Security: It refers to the security of the premises, and by so it's provided to the clients at the moment they visit, and it occurs, for example, when there's enough security personnel, the security zones are clearly stablished, when the escape routes are clearly marked, when you have medical kits, etc.

Hygiene: It refers to the hygiene and cleanness present in the premises and the employees, and it occurs, for example, when the bathrooms in the premises are always clean, there are no papers on the floor, when the employees are well neat, they wear uniform and dress impeccably, and have their nails cut, sort of speak.

A company or business gives out good client service when it has worked through all these different elements: for example, when they treat their clients kindly, they given them personal treatment, they attend fast, they offer them a comfortable environment, and makes them feel at ease and secure.

What's the importance of client service?

When clients find the products, they´re looking for and also receive good client service, they are satisfied and that makes them want to return and buy back from us, and most probably they'll recommend us with other people.

But, on the other hand, whether they find the product they look for or not, and they receive a terrible attention, they'll not only not visit us again, but they'll speak the worst of us and tell their experience to at least 9 or 20 people, depending on the level of displeasure.

It to this we add the fact that competition is increasing and the products they offer on the market are almost equal in quality and price, it's possible to say that nowadays is basic to provide an excellent client service if we want to be competitive on the market.

We must stop that the client is not well attended, so he doesn't stop visiting us or speaks hash about us. Better to procure them with an outstanding client service and get their loyalty, so we have good possibilities of being recommended with other customers, and we're able to be different form other competitors.

Good client service should be present in all the business' aspects in which there's client interaction, from the greeting from the security personnel at the door, to the phone call answered by the secretary. To what is necessary to constantly prepare and motivate the personnel, so they provide an excellent client service, not only to those employees that have constant contact with the clients, but all of those who can have it in a certain time, from the company's CEO to the cleaner.

Likewise, good client service must not only be provided at the moment of the sale, but also once it has been concreted.

Post-Sale Service

Post-Sale Service is the kind of service provided once the sale has been concreted.

Post-Sale Services are:

Promotional: Those related with sales promotion, and they occur, for example, when frequent clients get special discounts or offers, or when they're participating in raffles.

Psychological: Those that are linked to the client's motivation, and they occur, for example, when gifts, cards, and greeting cards are sent to them for their birthday or when you call them to ask them how they're doing with their product.

Security: Those that provide product purchase protection, and they occur, for example, when the clients receive purchase guarantees, or when the company has a return policy for defective products.

Maintenance: Those which involve maintenance or technical support service, and they occur, for example, when product installation service is provided, or when the training service is provided on its use-

"If you make a sale, it'll give enough for you to live. If you invest time and provide good client service, you can make a fortune." Jim Rohn

Providing a good post-sale service does not only allow us to get the benefits of providing good client service, such as the possibility the client's visits us again, or recommends us to other clients, but also gives us the possibility of keeping in touch and lengthen the relationship with the client, so, for example, get feedback from them, and let them know about our new products and promotions on interest.

Three maxims of customer service:

1. Apologize, don´t discuss: If a client has a problem, ask for forgiveness and solve the issue. Allow clients to air their complaints, even if you´re tempted in interrupting and correcting them, hold yourself back.

2. Ask for feedback, so you don´t lose your way: Ask your clients to grade your service periodically.

3. Be flexible: This means to make a project to a client, or to organize a reunion first thing in the morning.

Client Service is one of small companies' greatest strengths, and this can compete with the big companies.

"A COMPLAINT IS A GIFT of complaint to satisfaction."

The clients won´t trust you unless they get the results they're expecting, so something that'll help you as a sales tool is you give them a results' guarantee or give them their money back if they don't get them in a certain amount of time.

Is it too hard to offer this benefit to the client? It is so if you´re product or service is not the best, so if you have any doubts in being able to get them their results in a certain time, then don´t offer it, and make an improvement plan for all your products and services. This is going to be a n even stronger sales argument and that most of the world class companies are doing it as such.

Always give them more than they ask for. A results' guarantee is something that'll make your clients trust in your product or service but specially you as a sales person.

It's also important you have a client´s service department so you can keep attending and providing attention to your current clients.

Written **Results'** Guarantee, if by the end of **3 months**, the agreed result is not happening, so according to the agreement they get  their **money** back.

What's a Results' Guarantee?

A results' guarantee is to give your clients trust based on showing them you are so certain your products or services will get them the results in a certain period of time, that you even set a timing for it, so they can see it as such.

The parts a results' guarantee should have, are the following:

1. Whether is written: Give your client a standard time where you write down in the back the purchase date along with the client´s signature and name as approval. Make sure to include all these guarantees in a database where you have the dates all tied up.
2. Give out a limited time period: There's a time limit, and as there could be clients mistaken the actual date or that would try go over ready, in some cases. So, depending on your sales rate, as advice Is suggest you use, in the case of services, a 3-month guarantee. And regarding products, it would highly depend on the date of expiry and the products' life cycle. This time should be more than enough in order for you to ensure the results.
3. Make sure which the indicators or metrics are by which you're offering such guarantee. Here you can be able to be conscious about the causes for which you can accept product return. For example, in the case of a vacuum cleaner, give them a 6-month guarantee, knowing that's the time the product can endure under extreme conditions. In the case of a service company, as in my case, we give out a 3-month guarantee in order to be able to reach the productivity goals which we stablished since the beginning, for thanks to our experience, we know 3 months is the maximum time required to get the results.

Why is the guarantee so important?

It's for the client's trust in us, and I assure you, this will increase your sales up to 30%, and it will help your clients make a decision, as they know you're sure on the results you're offering them.

"Sales are a person to person **business. In the world** of professional sales, the real job starts **after the sale is done**." Jim Rohn

$uper Seller Powers

1. Write down a promise about the money return, so you're well known in the market for it.
2. Write down a procedure to request payments and let all your clients know about it.
3. Make a discount plan for prompt payment.
4. Evaluate thoroughly the guarantee you'll be offering, before you do, so you don't promise what you cannot meet.
5. Have the indicators ready before handing over the guarantees.
6. In your round table $uper Sellers' meeting, share the results' guarantee with them so they can give you feedback.

7. Let your business' results' guarantee be shown in all your publicity.

Who's the best Sales Person?

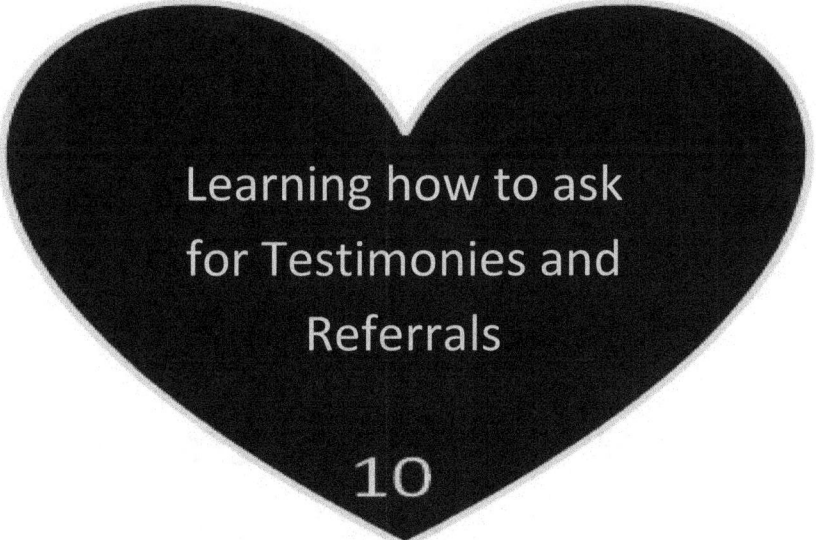

Learning how to ask for Testimonies and Referrals

10

"**The best sales person** in a **company** is a **satisfied client**, so learn to **capitalize** them, and when you do, remember to **reward them**." David Gaona

1. What's a testimony?
2. Why is it important to use testimonies?
3. How to use testimonies?
4. What's a referral?
5. Why is a referral plan important?
6. How to choose the right incentive?
7. $uper Seller Powers

What's a testimony?

It's basically a letter, video, writing, or email, where the client explains everything you helped them with, so your next clients buy your product or service. It's an art, you have to learn to use your satisfied clients to help other clients.

How to use client's testimonies as a sales strategy?

Companies survive thanks to client satisfaction, and this can be measured thanks to the testimonies you send them. Each product clients buy makes them happy to a certain point. In such cases, business owners can ask their very satisfied clients to send a testimony, which will have proof the about business people's credibility and the product's superiority, besides revealing other consumers prefer the product over many others. Of course, testimonies can only be used with previous notice.

"Good **service** will give **multiple sales.** If you treat your **clients** well, they will **open** doors you never could open yourself before." Jim Rohn

Testimonies are important as long as detailed and elaborated about the benefits of using the product. It's also adequate to use a catchy phrase from a client, which will get the buyer's attention, who are inclined to look at the testimonies before purchasing anything, so they won't make a mistake.

The following ways in using testimonies help products to be promoted and have shown to be an efficient marketing strategy:

a. Publish testimonies on your website, so all visitors read them, and you show them your satisfied customers, who have trusted your product.

b. Print testimonies in your business cards so they stand out. This can often influence potential clients and convince them your company is the best choice to fit their needs.

c. The testimony fragments can be part of an email signature which will highlight why they need to choose your company through all the competitor's network.

d. Testimonies can be part of your product boxes, while the presentation of these items and articles can increase the traffic in your website.

e. The news bulletin can have a special testimony section, so clients, more than reading the multiple testimonies, are even more convinced about the company or product your offering them.

f. Testimonies about certain profiles in social media sites like Facebook, and Twitter, are more efficient marketing strategies, thanks to the product benefits being able to reach a much larger audience through the social networks' channels.

g.   Testimonies give better results than any other sales copy and must be cited any place and or anywhere.

h.   Testimonies are the most powerful group and have a greater impact as the reader knows it's about a group of people who share the same good opinion about your company.

i.   Don´t alter or change any testimonies, so you can make the audience be familiar with the public opinion about your products and its benefits.

j.   The testimonies at fairs help you to improve public awareness about new products.

The message is clear: testimonies are nothing more than thankful words for the company and the products that you sale, but when used correctly, may result in one of the most efficient marketing techniques we possess, that come along with no extra charge, besides offering your clients the product or an impeccable service.

"Whatever you do, do it so well, they'll want to see it again and bring their friends along with them." Walt Disney

How to make a referral plan?

The clients' consumption habits have evolved and each day there are more sources of information that make them be more selective at the time of buying things.

More than just the product or price, there's an infinite number of important variables for decision making. However, today more than ever, our strategies in order to attract more clients and keeping them must be more effective.

Today, I share with you a simple strategy but powerful strategy in order to achieve this goal, and it's through the implementation of a compensation system for referrals.

In order to understand how this works, we need to remember that old business principle: "A satisfied customer attracts 5 or 10 new clients, meanwhile an unsatisfied customer will make you lose 10 or 15 potential clients."

This is still totally true today. Why? For two simple reasons:

1. Everyone as clients, recommend our buying experience as positive or negative. Just see, we all recommend our experience, and this has to do with the product, price, attention, and provider support. Every factor, in a certain measure, creates an experience, and that´s what we share mouth to mouth.

2. We all recommend stuff sooner or later, as an unconscious act, we all end up recommending out experience as buyers. Recommending is a natural human act. To talk about, whether we had a good or bad experience, it's only a way of expressing our feeling regarding that satisfying or frustrating moment.

So, we need to understand that sooner or later all our clients will talk about our business. They'll speak well or badly, so that, we can take advantage of this great impact as a strategy to attract more clients.

What's a referral plan?

Considering what's previously been said and assuming our clients will speak well of their experience with our business, we can exploit this impact in recommending, by rewarding our clients for referring us.

This fulfills two very positive effects:

1. Our client will feel motivated in speaking well about your business, continuing the positive experience, keeping your brand and company in his mind, which will sooner or later will make them come back. This is called client loyalty.

2. Our client will become a marketing medium attracting more potential clients through referrals.

So that, a referral plan can be summarized as a rewards system we offer our faithful clients for helping us attract other clients.

How does a referral program work?

It's even simpler than you can imagine. The first step consists in creating a good incentive that's attractive to your client, that motivates them to invite more clients to get to know your business or product.

This incentive or reward doesn't have to be very expensive, but can be small, though summed up in volume, they represent a benefit to your client seller.

Let's look at some examples:

1. 10% discount coupon in your next purchase for every client you refer us and buys from us. Perfect for: stores in general, furniture stores, tire sales, etc.

2. For each client you refer us and starts treatment, you'll receive a $20-dollar coupon for you to exchange on your next appointment. Perfect for: Medical Clinics, Dentists, Beauty Shops, Nutrition Centers, etc.

3. For each referred client that enlists with us, you receive a 50% discount on your monthly fee. Perfect for: Free Courses, Language Academies, Driving Schools, Training Centers, Cooking Schools, Cable Companies, Subscription Business, etc.

4. If you bring us a new client, will give a free service. Perfect for: Carwashes, Auto Shops, Office Cleaning, Computer Repair, etc.

How to pick the right incentive?

This is definitively the most complicated part, even though there´s really not much to lose but much to be won. Your client's personalities and the type of business you have, will determine the incentives to choose from. The common incentives may be:

1. Discounts on future purchases.
2. Mid-term Cumulative bonuses.
3. Free Services.
4. Discounts on services.

And the most important thing to consider are costs, for it'll be useless to offer large discounts blindfolded, if this will eat up your earnings, sort of speak. The rule which will determine if your referral program is rightfully focused, is that you always have to win as well as your client too.

For example, if you offer a $30-dollar discount as a reward, but you know first-hand this client will represent you $500 dollars on future sales, and let's say your net profit is 30%, means this new client will only represent you $150 dollars in your pocket. So, you're $30 dollars on rewards in order to obtain $150, this would be a well thought out profitable incentive.

Another example. If you have a Computer Repair Company and offer you client a free maintenance service as retribution, in exchange for a referral, we should do it like this. If the maintenance service costs $20 dollars, and that client will only buy from you a service of the same type for the same type of value of $30 dollars. Then, you're offering a $20-dollar reward in exchange for an estimated profit of $10 dollars. If you consider the material required to promote your program, this could be a wrongfully thought strategy, unprofitable, and that needs to be reconsidered.

Anyway, these are just some basic examples for you to understand how a referral system should be created as a strategy to attract clients.

Finally, you should promote your referral program. if you don't release it, no one will be interested. Due to this, you should destine a moderate percentage for an advertising budget, to inform your clients about your program, and it should describe clearly the following:

How does it work?

What are the rewards?

Who apply and who don't?

What are the restrictions?

When and how are the rewards collected?

You must emphasize on the feature that it's something fresh, great, and interesting for your clients. Phrases like "Now you win just by buying" or, "Earn lots of money by recommending your friends", and so on, are good strategies to call your clients attention.

So that, this is a very useful strategy and that planned out very adequately, can give you enormous benefits to expand your customer portfolio and increase your sales.

"The best sales person is always one of your most satisfied clients." David Gaona

What's the importance of referrals?

Lots of companies grow out of referrals, if one person had a good experience, he told another and so on. Referred clients are of the best quality for usually one you already know just did the job for you. Price is not the main problem, because who referred them already explained them the value it generates, and they have clear what they need.

So, how to attract more referred clients? It most cases it´s simply to include them in the commercial process and keep it present at all times.

"If you really get to impress them, your clients will tell this to many others. The word that circulates from mouth to mouth is very powerful." Jeff Bezos

You're not obtaining referrals?

When a company doesn't get the number of referrals they need, it's generally because:

1. They don't have the mindfulness to promote referrals, which is not something they have present in their commercial process or their client relationships.

2. They forget to ask for them or don´t know to do it naturally.
3. They don´t want to make their clients uncomfortable, or to feel bad, or seem desperate.
4. They're not sure their products or services are totally referable. They think they need to adjust some processes in order to improve the clients' experience.
5. Clients are not being satisfied with the job you've done or are just not giving anything to talk about.

When to ask for referrals?

There are better moments than others to request referrals. As a general rule, the best moment is when the client is surprised, thankful, and delighted about something special in your product or service.

Think about asking for referrals when:

1. Show something to your client or prospect.
2. Make your client or prospect think differently.
3. Solve or prevent a problem.
4. A prospect decides to become a client.
5. They achieve their first goal and it generates them results.
6. They're pleased for the job done.

When to ask for referrals?

There are better moments than others to request referrals. As a general rule, the best moment is when the client is surprised, thankful, and delighted about something special in your product or service.

Think about asking for referrals when:

7. Show something to your client or prospect.
8. Make your client or prospect think differently.
9. Solve or prevent a problem.
10. A prospect decides to become a client.
11. They achieve their first goal and it generates them results.
12. They're pleased for the job done.

How to ask for referrals?

After having done a really good job with your client, just ask them if they know other people or companies that could require the same solution that you provided to them. Think about all the added value that you've generated. Remember, you are not asking for a favor, you are letting that person help other people enjoy from the same advantages.

If you have that mentality, you will realize that you can request for referrals without bothering.

And a way to gratify them if by creating a referral program, think of creative ideas to offer not only to clients but to strategic allies (other companies who sell to your client, but are not your competition).

Referrals are the most profitable type of customers, so it is worth it to have a specific plan to promote them.

To many businesspeople, just the act of asking for referrals generates them anxiety. And I share that, there is nothing more uncomfortable that a salesperson who after we haven't manifested slight interest in their product, additionally tells us: "I understand, nevertheless, Could you please give me the name of three people I may contact? Needless to say, I find it inappropriate.

I don't know why they would think I would want to stop being friends with my contacts. Why would they consider that, if I don't know them, would recommend them to people that mean something in my life. The reason is very simple: I value too much my relationships as to send them an intense salesperson that I consider is not going to be of any benefit to them.

And probably this is the same principle in which we base the fact that we do not like asking for favors, we don't feel comfortable asking for help, as much as to people we know as to people we don't know. Being much stricter to those we know.

First offer referrals

Nevertheless, in many cases, it could be really important to our business accomplish a larger number of referrals coming from other companies, potential strategic allies. How to accomplish this without bothering? The answer is in two steps: 1) make sure your product or service adds value, and 2) first offer referrals.

In the first step, being sure that what you do really helps other people, makes their life more productive or solves them a problem, gives you peace of mind that you are not asking for a favor, but instead you could be helping people or business with your product or service.

If you consider that you are not in the capacity to add value, or either is not your target market or you need to rethink your business model, because without offering a tangible value, it is really difficult that someone will feel comfortable referring you.

Second, an excellent way to generate referrals is to offer referrals. In many cases,

In many cases, other outstanding companies that target the same market that you may be interested in promoting together. However, how to approach them if you do not know them personally or do not have the necessary confidence? Providing referrals.

Identify companies you would refer

I have experienced it in my own company. Since my job is to support small businesses in their marketing strategies, it is very common for them to additionally require other complementary services such as the design of their website, printing of advertising material, graphic design or email marketing. In order to be able to recommend companies that effectively serve them, I do an exhaustive job of identifying and evaluating companies that I could recommend for several months.

The way of approaching has been very simple: "Since some of my clients would require your services, I would like to know more into detail about your company and understand in which way could you provide added value to my clients". In many cases I have come to require their services just to try them without recommending them.

It goes without saying that this way of approaching without requesting anything in return has become an excellent marketing tool, since in most cases you get referrals back.

Why an unsatisfied client is important?

Long time ago I heard a sales guru called Brian Tracy who changed the way I saw how to handle a client's dissatisfaction. Basically what I comprehended was to take a dissatisfied client as an opportunity to win more than 20 clients, what do I refer with this?, that if you accomplish to turn over that bitter experience into an unforgettable one then you are going to be able to use this as a huge sales tool, even more so I assure you this client is going to recommend you with everyone he crosses by if you are able to switch that negative impression into a positive one.

As a $uper Seller you can do it, you just need to understand that this client is going to take 3 or 4 times more time than a regular client but believe me it is worth it.

I am going to set an example in the courses we provide at www.ucalle.com, there was one client who was not satisfied with our service and we began to realize he was talking bad about us, as a result when we went to talk to him, what he gave us was this 3 principal reasons:

1. The first one was that he felt really disappointed because in one of our workshops we hadn't finished all the pages from the workbook.
2. The book he had bought wasn't autographed and he wanted to have an autographed copy.
3. He hadn't liked the food we offered because he was vegan and we had only offered non-vegan protein.

Logically what we did was:

1. Sit with him to fully understand his complains, we listened, he explains with detail in almost 3 hours of talking, most companies don't pay attention to their dissatisfied clients they just give them their money back, but they don't go further into understanding the client's needs.
2. We wrote down all our clients complains and set a date to each one of them, we offered a free pass to another of our workshops and made sure that the workbook was 100%

completed, we gave him not one but 10 autographed books for him to recommend us with his friends.

3. We gave him a VIP pass and added into our menu vegan protein for people to order in anticipation.

What did we win?

Obviously our dissatisfied client became a fan of Universidad de la Calle an of our workshops, (you may log into www.ucalle.com to see all the courses and workshops we offer) he has recommended about 100 people in 6 months, so you must understand that from a dissatisfied client you can always learn and you have the opportunity to improve considerably if you give it the due importance.

Your most dissatisfied clients are your greatest learning source. Bill Gates

$uper Seller's Powers

1. Ask your principal satisfied clients for 5 referrals, tell them that you want to be able to help his friends.

2. Send your top 10 referral clients for their respective businesses.

3. Make a list of 10 people who can give you testimony and make sure you take video or bring a list of possible questions when interviewing them and tell them that you will use it to show as an example to other potential buyers.

4. Make a referral program, where you include what you will give each client that refers you.

5. Make a newsletter and send it by e-mail.

6. Enroll in chambers of commerce, financial groups or any type of

association where you can meet people who need your services.

7. Provide referrals to your main clients so they can do business.

Did you know Advertising can be an investment if you use it in the right measure?

Guerrilla

Marketing

11

"**Thinking** is the **most difficult** job there is. Maybe that's the reason why so many **people** practice it." Henry Ford

1. **What's Guerrilla Marketing?**
2. **Which elements are necessary for Guerrilla Marketing's Efficiency?**
3. **What are the 5 Steps of Guerrilla Marketing?**
4. **Why is it an advertising war?**
5. **Are you seeing opportunities in other places?**
6. **What are the 21 weapons in Guerrilla Marketing you can use now that you can start?**
7. **$uper Seller Powers**

What's Guerrilla Marketing?

This term usually receives attention for being so unconventional, even though it passes the very essence of every Marketing technique.

It's possible to define Guerrilla Marketing as a set of Marketing strategies and tools through less unconventional means which relevance is not to be considered advertisement as such, through wit, creativity, originality, and the element of surprise. It gives the audience an experience of intrigue, surprise and confusion that puts a smile on your face and makes you remember.

It requires a much more lower cost than conventional techniques and provides a maximum performance, consequence of the environment it creates and the way the message is created, far from being like the constant and tiring regular advertising bombings, becoming more outdated and littler renovated.

And, What elements are required for Guerrilla Marketing's Efficiency?

1. Using of creativity and innovation is basic, we cannot expect different results by doing the same thing.
2. Using unconventional means and technology as they're symbols of innovation.
3. It's possible to complement it to other traditional Marketing Techniques.
4. You need to connect with the users, provide them with a moment comfortable and amazing moment they can remember.

It powers the skill to create a new client relationship, but not so much in pursing the product's features. Remembering a great and impressive experience you lived will create interest in getting back such experience through searching and acquiring the product or service. Besides, the client will feel bonded to the company.

This term usually receives interest for being unconventional, even though it passes on the very essence of from these marketing techniques.

What the 5 Steps in Guerrilla Marketing?

1. Stablish clear, brief, and concise objectives.

You need to decide on what objectives, your guerrilla marketing strategy, like selling 30% more on a certain date, increasing the traffic number on your website, increasing your amount of contacts on social networks, you decide. But the important thing is you set a written goal in a structured way.

2. Define your target market.

You need to know who to sale to, you have to define who your potential clients are, you have to be clear on what kind of people you need to reach to. It they're adults, between what ages, their likes, education, what jobs they perform, where they live, this will help your Guerrilla Marketing Strategy be very focused in obtaining the best results.

3. Study your target market.

Once you know who your potential clients are, now it´s the moment to study you target market's behavior, that you know what they like, their income, favorite places, if they have a family, if they're married or single, what food do they like, the clothes they wear, the artist they enjoy, and so on. Get the biggest amount of information you can in order to make you Guerrilla Marketing and get the best result possible being very focused.

4. Develop a strategy.

Once you have the study then you have to think in a low budget strategy where the least expensive strategy gets to the most quantity possible, that's Guerrilla Marketing. You can use from including your electronic signature in each email you send, including your logos in your car, giving out stickers with phrases to your clients, giving out conferences in order to prospect in crowded places, make raffles on social networks, using keywords to position your website. You need to make a brainstorm where you start thinking in what type of advertisement to use in order to attract more clients to your business without investing that much.

Everything should say absolutely everything and must be of low budget. For me, a Guerrilla Marketing budget shouldn't be more than 1 thousand dollars, though it's recommended you use 10% of your income for your business advertising. The first thing I want you to do is find the exact mix and formula for your business to have more clients without using too much money.

Then, the first step is to assign a low budget, and number two, start making a brainstorm in order to try out everything that works out well, and obviously stop using what doesn't. So, now the task if you sit down now and write down all the possible low budget ways to advertise your business and remember to ask 4 or 5 people to do the same for you, so they give you a list about what they think could attract you more clients.

5.   Value and measure the results.

The most important thing here is to test each tool. What I can say is I have found lots of impressive results on clients, I tell you, I have a client who invested 20 years on Television advertisement, which he called investing, but when we did the Return of Investment (ROI), it was a great surprise to know the amount of people coming thanks to those $50 thousand dollars were from 30 to 40 people a month. Imagine all that money wasted for not measuring every sales tool. What you'll be doing in Guerrilla Marketing is different than anything else. As pointless it may seem, you must analyze how much it's generating and where do all the people who enter your store and purchase a product come from.

Why?

Once we know the exact combination in order to attract more clients and know the most efficient tool for that, then we have to make a bigger investment, and like Seth Godin always says, "se have to buy more clients."

Buying clients means you have to pay more advertising, which need to be direct results from your business sales.

Why is it a war?

You have to understand that being a business person is so much like being in a war. You need to be using weapons and tools for you to conquer and you have to travel to new territories. You need to be in constant awareness, you have to train and always be awaken in order to fight your enemies. You have to be recruiting adepts for your army, you have to improve all the time for what once worked out for you, I assure you, won´t work forever.

You have to work really hard for the enemy is always studying you to get what you have, you need to be the general and you´re in charge or making things happen and you'll be at war the whole time. So, get to work, and find the formula for you to buy more clients and always be ready to change your advertising strategy once you find out this one doesn't work.

You're at war.

"**Marketing** is being transformed into a **war** based more on **information** than in the power of sales." Philip Kotler

You have to understand that Guerrilla means choosing what tactic, it means you'll do it silently and with a methodology most people wouldn't find to be traditional nor expect it. Your clients will never see you coming, but it will reach them from everywhere, but in the same time, it must be a strategy that helps position your brand in a very professional way and at a very low cost. Remember to measure everything and make sure it has Return of Investment (ROI). Also make sure to see the competition and make an analysis of what is it they do and how they do it, so you can imitate them, and most importantly, try whatever it is they´re doing. Also check on other people who are in similar businesses and imitate them, but the most important thing is you proof that whatever it is they´re doing, actually works. This is called Street Guerrilla.

"If you think **Advertising** doesn't work, consider all the million people that now believe **Yogur** is **delicious**." Joel Whiltley

Are you seeing opportunities everywhere?

As a strategist and a $uper Seller you must be very aware of possible opportunities, because they're everywhere. Take a pen and notebook with you and write down everything that comes to your mind as well as everything you picture for advertising and possible prospects. Don't leave anything out, better write it down, even though memory is useful, I assure you it's not as effective as writing it down, and you sit down at night to make real everything you wrote down, or as a part of plan. Write everything down, and everything means everything.

Once you have tried all conventional methods, it´s important you also make an internet plan, which is something that always works. Just as in Guerrilla Marketing, you have to try all things. You have to research about doing internet advertisements. First do research and test every campaign you do. There are pretty cheap methods and your return of investment is very profitable. There are others that only help you position your brand, but what's important is you test them. I recommend you get advice from someone with experience in what you're looking for attracting clients by internet.

"Everything is about **trying things** out and see if they **work**." Ray Bradbury

I'm sure you´re very smart, and that you can accomplish many things by yourself, but I think they best way of getting somewhere is by getting advice from people who already did what you hope to achieve. There's 5 Steps in order for you to do what you want.

1. Be aware of what you want to accomplish as a $uper Seller.
2. Imitate someone who already did what you want to achieve and pay that person to train you.
3. Mass Action.
4. Correct what's not working out.
5. Never stop until you achieve your goal.

The term "Scratch my back" is you to have someone who can do what you can't by your side. Somebody who completes the advertising topic. Even though you're a $uper Seller, it's very possible you don't have the skills to produce advertisements, so you need to have someone work for you who is an expert on the subject.

Hire a coach, remember it's not how much it costs to have a coach, but how much have you missed out on earning for not having them. We are experts in helping you fulfill your goals in record time. Contact us at www.iexito.com and we'll be able to give you advise on how to reach your goals as soon as possible.

Now, I'm going to give you 21 methods you can use to start your Guerrilla Marketing right away. The most certain thing is you already have a method, and if you do so, then complete it, but remember, that each person that enters your business and buys your product or service, you have to know by which method did they arrive to you. Measure, measure, and with this make decisions and remember the only constant in life is change, so change your methodology until it works.

Which are the 21 weapons in Guerrilla Marketing you can start using now?

1. Put an ad from your business in your business.
2. Put an ad in your car that has a phone number.
3. Include logo and your business pages in the email's signature.
4. Business cards in every page and telephone.
5. Doing half pages where you explain your business and pass on to possible clients.
6. Doing webpages.
7. Putting posters in points of sale.
8. Send an email to all your database.
9. Send a WhatsApp message to all your contacts.
10. Send Facebook messages offering your services.
11. Send invites to all your Facebook contacts.
12. Google Ad Works Advertisements.
13. Making YouTube Videos.
14. Getting Databases from the Yellow Pages.
15. Post in business pages.
16. Make a recommendation plan for clients.
17. Visit Chambers of Commerce to place advertisements.
18. Make a Power Point presentation explaining your services and upload it to Slide Share.
19. Create a Facebook page.
20. Create a Twitter page.
21. Call all the contacts you have on your phone.

"Retailers, wholesalers, and logistics organizations all need their **Marketing** strategies."
Philip Kotler

What's the formula in order to measure how much does a client cost?

You need to know how much it costs to attract a new client. It's important to understand and analyze this information the whole time, for how much you'll assign to the sales budget depends on it, and most importantly, you'll know what's the most effective way to attract clients to your company.

You need to have the following information:

1. Knowing where each client comes from. For example, this month we sold 100 products or services to new clients. Here it´s important to eliminate the says you already have so you don´t misinterpret the information. 20 came though the panoramic ad, 30 by the webpage, 10 by the radio, and through social networks.
2. You need to have the info on how much you sold with these 100 clients. Here is when you add all sales. Let's suppose you sold $100 clients with these 100 clients, and at the same time, you need to know how much you sold through every advertisement mean you used. For example, you sold $50,000.00 dollars though referrals, through panoramic ad $10 thousand dollars, through webpage 10 thousand dollars, through the radio 20 thousand, and through social media 10 thousand dollars.
3. Now, you're going to determine the total advertising costs of all the five means you used and how much did each recommendation cost. Let's suppose it cost you 1 thousand dollars, the cost for a panoramic ad is 10 thousand dollars, the webpage cost 5 thousand dollars, the radio spot cost 10 thousand dollars, and the social media cost 4 thousand dollars, so you defined that your total cost is 30 thousand dollars.

With al this information you have the **IXNC** (Investment per new client), that can be calculated very simply, just divide 30 thousand dollars in 100 clients.

IXCN (Advertisement Costs/New Clients)

IXCN = 30 thousand dollars / 100 clients = 300 hundred dollars per client

Prepare your Advertising Budget

You must destine at least 10% of your income each month to advertisements. So many companies never invest in advertisements, which determines if you're a big company or just one from the bunch. As a $uper Seller, you also need to become a future Business Person, for when you acquire the sales skill, you already have the most difficult to acquire. As a business person, you need 4 skills we already talked about. First sales, then leadership, management, and fourth investment. You please need to learn to do advertisements, assign a budget and ask for it constantly.

Do it now

Stop postponing things, do now what you have to do in order to increase sales. What I ask of you is to assign and do the budget, just do what you have to do in order to achieve your goals. Repeat to yourself constantly, do it now, do it now, do it now.

We all count with 24 hours, us that earn up to $100 thousand dollars a month, as well as the ones who have trouble paying for their bills. It all depends on what you do in free time and the action you take, so act now and do it now. Take the time and act, but never stop till you get to your goal and test everything you do.

Why do you need to learn from your mistakes?

 The key is you try out many things and measure them making adjustments all the time. Learn from your mistakes. I can tell you I've made lots of mistakes in Marketing and my businesses, but the most important thing is to learn from them. It doesn't matter if you keep making mistakes, but that they're now even more before, this is important. Like Mr. Carlos Slim says, if you're going to make mistakes, make a lot of them, so keep on trying, but the important thing is not to make the same mistakes. Just keep learning and training yourself until you get what you want.

"If you're going to make **mistakes**, make sure to make **big ones**, but don´t make the **same ones**." Carlos Slim

$uper Seller Powers

1. Make a list of all the possible Marketing and Advertisement strategies to use with no cost.
2. Make a list of all the possible Marketing and Advertisement strategies to use with cost.
3. Calculate the investment per client.
4. Make a list of the biggest mistakes you've made and what was it you learned regarding advertising.
5. Look for someone to advice you on advertising.
6. Learn from the competition, check out what they're doing and copy what's working for them.
7. Do it now, please act on it, and learn from your mistakes.

Did you know that what determines your success mostly is the action you take after learning something?

Now what?

12

"It is not **what you know** but what you **do** with what you know what is going to get you to your **goals**." David Gaona

POWER =

Information +

Action

The system never fails, if you apply it and you do it with massive action you are going to notice that you are going to obtain amazing and outstanding results. So you need to get out and do it.

Your list of shores is 7:

1. Hire a coach to help you obtain what you want faster. You may hire the best of the world at www.iexito.com.
2. Keep training it is really important that you maintain your energy through courses. Go to the experiential workshop Sales Machine to live what you've just read in this book.
3. Buy more sales books, I gave you a list from the ones I use as a personal library.
4. Apply everything you have learned without overthinking it, the next two weeks are fundamental. Use the CIPASA.
5. Learn the closings by heart.
6. Improve your environment, clean your room and make yourself as efficient as possible.
7. Everyday make the 5 most important things to sell more.

Most importantly make your own system

This system works I have used it for many years, besides I have copied it from the biggest salesmen worldwide to the $uper Sellers, but I want you to take it and make it your own, make the necessary modifications and document it. You must improve it, but only once you have become an expert at it. Thank you and congratulations for finishing the book and now it is time for action.

See you soon in the workshops and thank you for buying this book.

Thank you!

Conclusions

In this life everything is a sale, either someone is selling to you or you are selling to them, make sure you train your whole life to be the best salesperson you can be. Remember that selling is a tool that is going to be helpful in every aspect of your life, either familiar, sentimental, business, sports, socially, so learn the steps of the CIPASA system and become an expert. Amaze yourself with all the blessings you are going to bring into your life by knowing how to sell and you are going to realize day by day that it becomes easier and above all you are going to enjoy it even more, learn the tools by heart and use them.

Keep training yourself, buy books and audio books, go to courses and workshops, always improve, don't use money or time excuses, remember there are only EXCUSES OR RESULTS!, success never has excuses so go get everything that you want. Remember that the information that gets inside your brain is never going to get out of there and becomes an asset, find yourself a coach and pay them, never spare in your mental, spiritual and physical training, it has been my main investment for me for 10 years now. Never spare in your education, don't doubt it keep on training.

Go get your dreams and never give up.

¡EXCUSES

OR

RESULTS!

A $uper Seller's code of honor

I AM a $uper Seller and I Always help my clients.

I AM an excellent problem solver.

I always enjoy the sales.

I AM a money magnet.

I always attract clients and people that want to do business with me.

I always think that everybody should win.

I never give up.

I train and read all the time.

I improve all the time.

I am a God's instrument to serve.

Bibliography

The psychology of selling, Brian Tracy

The art of closing the sale, Brian Tracy

Sales Dogs, Blair Singer

Unlimited sales power, Donald Moine

The greatest salesman in the world, Og Mandino

Swim with sharks without being eaten alive, Harvey B. Mackay

Sales for dummies, Tom Hopkins

Superstar sales, Tom Hopkins

How to master the art of selling, Tom Hopkins

How to gain friends and influence in other people, Dale Carnegie

Secrets of closing the sale, Zig Ziglar

Guerrilla marketing, Jay Conrad Levinson

What everybody is saying, Joe Navarro

Seller's Prayer

My Lord, Creator of all things, thanks for always helping me keep my goals in mind.

Thank you for the ability to take advantage of my opportunities and teach me how to conquer with words and to thrive with love.

Thank you for helping me to live today as if it were the last and to guide my words so that they are fruitful and to help me discipline in order to never give up.

Thank you for opening my eyes to see every opportunity and for enriching me with good habits and for giving me patience and persistence to achieve each goal that I set for myself.

Thank you for helping me to sell more of my products and services, either by phone, online or in person and to do it in a simple and fluid way because my clients and prospects answer me easily and constantly look for me to obtain more of my products.

Thank you for helping us to sell more and more of our products and with them to help more and more people and to open more and more doors and provide us with more markets around the world.

Thank you for helping us to increase sales with our current customers and to increase our customer base in a smooth, easy manner and by recommendation.

Thank you for helping us meet and exceed the needs of our customers and that they become our best sellers due to our excellent service.

I thank you for everything you give me and what is yet to come because I know that I owe to you all the success and that's why I thank you and execute every action knowing that you guide me in every step.

www.ingramcontent.com/pod-product-compliance
Lightning Source LLC
Chambersburg PA
CBHW072132170526
45158CD00004DA/1341